MW00625950

REMEMBERING

A HISTORY OF
SOUTHERN OREGON UNIVERSITY

REMEMBERING

A HISTORY OF
SOUTHERN OREGON UNIVERSITY

BY ARTHUR KREISMAN

UNIVERSITY OF
OREGON
PRESS

Produced by the Southern Oregon University Office of Publications:

Managing Editor: Melissa L. Michaels

Editor: Gary Kliewer

Editorial Assistant: Kiera Heston

Design: Gregory Martin

© 2002 University of Oregon Press
Published in conjunction with the Southern Oregon University Foundation

All rights reserved. No part of this book may be reproduced in any form without written permission from the publisher.

The opinions expressed in this book are those of the author and do not necessarily represent the views of Southern Oregon University.

Published by the University of Oregon Press
5283 University of Oregon
Eugene, OR 97403-5283
www.uopress.com

Manufactured in the United States of America
First edition, 2002

ISBN: 0-87114-079-9

TABLE OF CONTENTS

THROUGH THE YEARS

1872 .... Ashland Academy .... AA

1878 .... Ashland Academy and Commercial College .... AACC

1879 .... Ashland College and Normal School .... ACNS

1887–90 .... Ashland State Normal School .... ASNS

1895–1909 .... Southern Oregon State Normal School .... SOSNS

1926 .... Southern Oregon State Normal School .... SOSNS

1932 .... Southern Oregon Normal School .... SONS

1939 .... Southern Oregon College of Education .... SOCE

1956 .... Southern Oregon College .... SOC

1975 .... Southern Oregon State College .... SOSC

1997 .... Southern Oregon University .... SOU

FOREWORD

AS THE TENTH PRESIDENT of Southern Oregon University, I am honored to introduce the first comprehensive history of this remarkable university. It is evident from *Remembering: A History of Southern Oregon University* that I am succeeding a line of stellar presidents whose dedication to the University was marked by extraordinary passion, integrity, and enthusiasm. It is my challenge and my delight to follow in the footsteps of such legendary leaders as the commanding Julius Churchill, the charismatic Elmo Stevenson, and the gregarious Stephen Reno, while also adding my own footprints and pathways into the future for the University.

And yet these were not the only individuals who have kept this institution thriving over the years. These pages will introduce you to many of our exceptional faculty and staff, from "oldtimers" Marion Ady, Angus Bowmer, Roy McNeal, Arthur Taylor, and Wayne Wells to the "newcomers" of 1946—including Arthur Kreisman, university historian, emeritus professor, and the author of this book; Harold

Bishop, who coined the term "Pear Bowl" during his tenure as athletic director; and Leon Mulling, emeritus professor of speech-communication who has contributed generously to the Institution, both in the form of service and scholarships—and on through our current crop of esteemed faculty and staff. Today, we continue the legacy of student-centered education and sterling service established more than a century ago with the first incarnation of the School in 1872.

The University has always enjoyed a fruitful and satisfying relationship with the local communities, which repeatedly rallied to its aid when the Institution's funding was threatened. In return, Southern's faculty, staff, and students have contributed to the culture, economy, and intellectual development of the region. As you will see in *Remembering*, our faculty members have played significant roles in the founding and support of such flagship organizations as the Oregon Shakespeare Festival, the Mount Ashland Ski Lodge, Britt Festivals, and the Pacific Northwest Museum of Natural History. The College also helped land the National Fish and Wildlife Forensics Laboratory in Ashland, and it is host to the award-winning Jefferson Public Radio. These and other local agencies have provided a hands-on training ground for our students, and more than 80 percent of our alumni continue to live and work in the state of Oregon. This collaborative exchange between an institution and the local communities is one of the distinguishing characteristics of a successful university, and we are grateful to the city of Ashland for supporting the Institution from the beginning. We are also excited to witness the ever-increasing engagement of the communities north and south of us. The international representation on campus today is another sign of progress, marked especially by the unique relationship with our sister city of Guanajuato, Mexico, and its Universidad de Guanajuato.

Throughout its history, the Institution has experienced various budgetary and political setbacks. Nevertheless, Southern has always emerged as a survivor, reinventing (and renaming!) itself several times over, and it celebrated its seventy-fifth anniversary of uninterrupted service in 2001 (dating back to the "third incarnation," which opened in 1926). The Institution received university status in 1997, when Southern Oregon State College (SOSC) became Southern Oregon University. Not long before that, the Oregon University System (OUS) had designated the Institution a Center of Excellence in the Fine and Performing Arts. Although the journey from two-story wooden schoolhouse to contemporary university was marked by economic adversity, the campus community has continually displayed tremendous commitment to the mission and values of our great institution.

As Adlai Stevenson remarked in a 1952 speech, "We can chart our future clearly and wisely only when we know the path which has led to the present." Art Kreisman's meticulous account provides precisely the historical context we need as we formulate our vision for the next era of the University. We honor our forebears by studying their scholarship, involvement, and growth. This history can serve as an instructive model not only for the SOU community, but also for the broader local, national, and international communities. We invite you to join us in this voyage from Ashland Academy to Southern Oregon University, as we chart our future to a contemporary public liberal arts and sciences university for Oregon.

Elisabeth Zinser, President

March 2002

INTRODUCTION

IT HAS BEEN MY PLEASURE and privilege to have served at Southern Oregon University since 1946. In that time, I have played various roles and promoted many initiatives. I have witnessed both good times and bad. First among the good was the opportunity to teach a host of wonderful students who were anxious to learn and willing to work hard. Second was the chance to know and work with many fine colleagues.

Among the bad were the constant struggles to obtain adequate financing and the frequent need to cut back our activities. There was also the occasional tragedy that struck people I admired and liked. One of the saddest duties I ever faced was preaching the memorial service for Dr. Elmo Stevenson, one of nature's true noblemen and a man I had come to love.

Over the years, however, the happy times have far outnumbered the sad ones.

It has been a joy to work on this history, and I have learned a great deal in the process. I have been as accurate and objective as possible. SOU is an excellent regional university, far better than many institutions with great reputations. There are faculty and staff members who could easily work at any school in the country, but— fortunately for us—they like it here. They really do keep everything here running, and running right. The buildings are in good shape, the grounds are lovely, the library is orderly, and the clerical work leaves nothing to be desired. All is done that needs to be done.

This community is a very special one. Ashland has always sup- ported higher education, and over the years the city has managed to do whatever was required to keep the Institution going. That is no small thing. We have been truly blessed in many, many ways.

This history is dedicated to all those who have given of them- selves unstintingly to help make SOU the fine institution that it is.

Arthur Kreisman | *Ashland, Oregon*

THE NINETEENTH
CENTURY AND THE FIRST
INCARNATION

IN 1850, THERE WERE ONLY 13,300 people in the entire Oregon Territory—which then included portions of Washington and Idaho. Ashland had not yet been founded. In 1852, a small group of people came into the Rogue Valley and settled by Lithia Creek, around what is now Ashland's downtown plaza. Slowly, a community developed. The 1860 U.S. Census lists 327 people in Ashland, and by 1869, citizens of the community were discussing the possibility of building an academy for the advanced education of the area's young people.

In 1884, A. G. Walling published a *History of Southern Oregon,* in which he wrote, "the Ashland College and Normal School was inaugurated in 1869 at a quarterly conference of the Methodist Episcopal Church held in Ashland in June of that year." (*Normal school* is the traditional name for a teacher-training academy.) Since 1884, all historical accounts of the College have begun with this information from Walling, ascribing the beginnings of the College to the Methodist Church. The problems with that statement are many. First, there was no Methodist Episcopal Church in Ashland until 1875. (The Methodist Episcopal Church became the United Methodist Church in 1937, when the northern and southern churches finally healed the rift caused by the Civil War.) Before then, circuit-riding preachers operating out of Jacksonville served Ashland Methodists. Further, the 1869 Methodist quarterly conference was held in Roseburg, not Ashland.

Walling was writing a type of book that could be called subscription history. He would visit a community, talk to people, get the names of all the important families, and then mention them in his book so they would all want to buy it.

In 1869, Ashland was a town of approximately 500 people. By the time Walling was walking its streets, Ashland probably had more than 1,000 people. Most of them simply didn't know the beginnings of the Ashland College, and they probably assumed that since the Methodist Episcopal Church was running the College at the time, it must always have been so. However, there are newspaper reports indicating that a group of Ashland citizens, already banded together under the name of the Rogue River Valley Educational Society, met on April 12, 1869, to consider building an academy. There is no way of knowing when this group had formed, but by May there were reports of subscribed money, the election of a board of directors, and the decision to begin working. On June 8, 1869, a site on the north side of town was selected, and a building committee was chosen, consisting of A. G. Rockfellow, J. W. Kuykendall, J. M. McCall, J. P. Walker, and J. H. Russell. It is true that most of these men were Methodists—at that time, it was the only organized church in

Ashland. But it is also clear that there was no official church presence in that original organization, although J. W. Kuykendall was one of the Methodist ministers in the area serving the Ashland congregation. For the most part, the organizers were public-spirited farmers and businessmen with great hopes for their community and for education.

The site selected for the academy was located where Briscoe School now stands. That land was part of an original Donation Land Claim of 320 acres claimed by one of the original settlers of Ashland, Abel Helman, who had come from Ashland County, Ohio. In 1850, Congress passed the Donation Land Claim Act, which allowed married settlers to take up to 640 acres and single settlers to claim 320 acres. Helman's land (Claim Number 40) consisted of parts of Sections 4, 5, 8, and 9 in Township 39 south of Range One East. Although the government did not deliver the official deed to that Donation Land Claim until 1865 (with the signature of President Andrew Johnson), it is clear that the possessors of such land felt secure in their titles to it, because Abel Helman sold the south half of his claim (160 acres) to his brother, John R. Helman, for $1,260 on April 20, 1858.

Actually, the story of the land is more complicated yet. Abel Helman owned the Ashland Flouring Mill—standing at the current entrance to Lithia Park. Apparently, he ran into a cash-flow problem and needed money. In 1856, he borrowed $750 for three months from L. J. C. Duncan at 7.5-percent interest per month (that amounts to 90-percent interest per year!). Helman was not able to repay that loan from Duncan. Sheriff Pyle sold the land to Duncan at a public auction (the south half of Claim Number 40) on May 29, 1958, for $2,150. But Abel had already sold the south half to his brother, John. It is unclear how this was finally resolved, based on remaining records. However, there is a record of a quitclaim deed for $5 from

L. J. C. Duncan to John Helman for the south half of Claim 40, dated February 18, 1859. Somehow, the debt Helman owed Duncan must have been satisfied.

Ten years later, the Rogue River Valley Educational Society began building its academy on Lots 1 and 2 of Block 7 in the south half of Claim 40. The *Oregonian* reported in May 1869 that $3,000 had been subscribed toward the building, while other sources reported that $1,700 had been raised. It is probable that $3,000 was the goal, and $1,700 the amount actually raised. Materials were purchased and building contracts were let to two young Ashland carpenters, Henry S. Emery and Christian F. Blake. Construction began in July 1869, but it came to a halt due to insufficient funds. Over a year later, more funds came in, and it was reported in September 1870 that "work on the Academy was again resumed this week and the job will be pushed ahead as fast as possible." But again, the money ran out. The next reference to the Ashland Academy does not appear until February 1872, when it was reported that "our Academy building, which has 'hung fire' for quite a while, is likely to be completed soon—an offer having been made by a gentleman to open a school in the building, when, if accepted, the necessary repairs will be made."

The gentleman was the Reverend Joseph Henry Skidmore, a remarkable individual born in England in 1837. He was the youngest of nine children born into a coal-mining family, none of whom could read or write. He went to work in a coal mine at the age of eight. Several years later, he accompanied his father and two sisters to Prince Edward Island, Canada, and, after less than a year, he moved to Providence, Rhode Island. He apprenticed as a stonecutter and marble carver for six years. Skidmore then decided he wanted an education, and he started school while working part time. At the

Reverend Joseph Henry Skidmore and Annie Hill Skidmore, founders of the Ashland Academy

age of twenty, he entered the Greenwich Academy, completing the equivalent of a high school education. His youngest son, Charles Evan Skidmore, stated in 1955 that his father then went to Wesleyan College in Middletown, Connecticut. However, Wesleyan (now University) has no record of a J.H. Skidmore. This may or may not be meaningful; records do get lost. In any event, he was converted to Methodism and became a teacher and a preacher. Skidmore went to California in 1863 and organized public schools in San Bernardino. He then moved to Oregon and engaged in logging for a while at Coos Bay. In 1868 and 1869, he served as a faculty member at the Wilbur Academy in Wilbur, just north of Roseburg.

In those days, Oregon's premier institution of higher learning was Willamette University, managed by the Methodist Episcopal Church. Methodist ministers developed a series of academies around Oregon to serve as feeders for Willamette. Wilbur Academy,

The Ashland Academy building

also known as Umpqua Academy, was one such institution, and it had official church status.

Reverend Skidmore—who had been admitted on trial to the Oregon Conference of the Methodist Church in 1868—met Annie Hill while teaching at Wilbur Academy. They married on July 6, 1869. The following year, Rev. Skidmore was given full membership in the Oregon Conference. In 1871, he was assigned to the Jacksonville Circuit, which also served Ashland. It was at this time that Rev. Skidmore met the Ashlanders who were trying to build the Ashland Academy. Although it is uncertain whether he approached them or they him, someone proposed that he take over the enterprise as a private endeavor. On March 13, 1872, John R. Helman and his wife sold Lots 1 and 2 of Block 7 to Rev. Skidmore for one dollar. By July 6, it was noted that "the Academy building [was] approaching rapidly to completion." And on July 20, it was reported in the press that "all persons who subscribed money or material for building the Academy have transferred their claims to the Principal, Rev. J.H. Skidmore, who is now sole proprietor."

The Skidmores moved to Ashland and were joined by Annie's father, Hancel C. Hill, who assisted his son-in-law with getting the Academy underway. Hill later became mayor and one of Ashland's leading citizens, serving for years on the Ashland City Council. But more funds were needed than the family was able to provide, and Rev. Skidmore had to borrow money from W.C. Myer, a prominent Ashlander who bred prize horses, in order to complete the building and open the School. According to Skidmore's son, Charles, Myer loaned the money at a 1-percent monthly interest rate.

The Academy building was a two-story wooden structure, but its size is a bit of a mystery. In a report to the state superintendent of public instruction for 1879–80, the building is described as being eighty-eight feet by sixty-four feet, with six schoolrooms and four "redi" rooms on five acres. An 1882 report to the state superintendent, however, described the building as seventy by fifty-eight feet, with four schoolrooms and four "redi" rooms on four acres. It would seem that there was a considerable shrinkage problem, or someone did not measure very well. The report also stated that the value of the property rose from $7,000 in 1879–80 to $8,000 in 1882.

The opening of the School was originally scheduled for the first Monday in October 1872, but Rev. Skidmore had to go East to purchase furnishings, which were described by one reporter as "elegant." These included sixty black walnut desks made in Chicago and brought in at a "handsome cost." The School finally opened on November 4, 1872. An advertisement for the Academy listed tuition per term as $4 for primary, $5 for preparatory, $6 for sub-junior, and $8 for senior. There were a variety of "extras." The School taught languages for $3 each, painting for $10, music for $10 (use of an instrument was an additional $3), and bookkeeping for $3 (single-entry) and $6 (for double-entry, of course). Board with private families cost $3.50 per week, "exclusive of washing." By December, 130 "scholars" were reported in attendance, and in January 1873, 150 were reported. These figures are misleading. One report (fall 1875) says the School opened with 50 students. In January 1877, 300 students were reported, but in September 1877, school opened with "over 60 in attendance." The reports and records of this period show that students could come and go at will. It would seem that, despite the "official" opening, one could come and start at any time, or drop out. It is likely that no one knew the actual enrollment at any given time.

Students also covered the spectrum from primary grades to college level. At the "advanced" level, the men formed a debating society called "The Rising Star," which in 1873 focused on the question,

"Resolved that navigation has done more for the benefit of the world at large than the art of printing." The women of the Academy also formed a club, which they named "The Casket of Jewels."

The original faculty consisted of Elizabeth Brooks of Jacksonville, who taught music; Lily Davis "from the Eastern states," who taught bookkeeping, drawing, and assisted with "classic recitations"; Annie Skidmore, who was in charge of the primary department; and Rev. Skidmore, who taught all the advanced courses. There is no report or record of salaries. By 1875, William T. Leeke had taken charge of the Commercial Department of the Academy, and Della Webber was in charge of the Music Department and taught German. Leeke resigned his position in April 1876 and was replaced by C. Merritt, but Leeke returned in January 1877. Meanwhile, it must have been difficult to muster enough students, because by the fall of 1876, advertisements for the Ashland Academy indicated that "scholars may enter at any time. Tuition charged only for time in attendance." In 1877, Skidmore reported having "top students" in university algebra, chemistry, natural philosophy, bookkeeping, music, and German. This gives some idea of the advanced curriculum.

In 1878, disaster struck. Apparently, the Academy had been kept afloat by a contract that Skidmore had with the city of Ashland, whereby he taught all Ashland students above the primary level. In early April, a public-school decision to rescind that contract left Skidmore without sufficient funding to continue the School. In addition, it is clear that many owed him money for past services, because he placed a notice in the paper saying that he had given his accounts to a local attorney to collect. The burden was too much; he could no longer keep up with his loan payments. In May 1878, the newspaper reported that Skidmore had rented out the Academy, and shortly thereafter, he left town.

Rev. Skidmore went to Roseburg, and in fall 1878, he took over for a short time as principal at Umpqua Academy in Wilbur. In 1880, he was readmitted to the Methodist ministry. He worked as principal at Sheridan Academy and, in 1882, as principal of Olympia Academy in Washington—both Methodist institutions. He later served churches in Idaho, Washington, and Oregon, until he passed away on May 2, 1916, in Vancouver, Washington.

Meanwhile, in Ashland, leadership of the Academy was assumed by William T. Leeke, who had been the commercial instructor, together with L. F. Willits and J. Q. Willits. In May 1878, the three incorporated the Institution as the Ashland Academy and Commercial College, with Leeke as president. They planned three programs of study: preparatory, academic, and commercial, with an added specialty in instrumental music. Leeke was listed as professor of mathematics. Rev. J. H. Vandever was professor of Latin and Greek. Kate Thornton was principal of the Intermediate Department. J. Q. Willits was professor of instrumental and vocal music, and Luella McBride taught painting and drawing. Tuition payment was requested in advance.

School began in September 1878. On November 22, 151 students enrolled. But just a week later, the Academy was in "financial trouble." The *Ashland Tidings* reported that the business was all right, but the building and grounds were heavily mortgaged. Stock was sold in order to purchase the property. This effort must have been unsuccessful, because in February 1879, the sheriff put the Academy up for sale and sold it to the only bidder, W. C. Myer, for $3,700, which covered the mortgages and legal costs. Myer, of course, was the person who had made the original loan to Rev. Skidmore. Apparently, the Leeke-Willits group was allowed to complete the school year, but it was unable to come to satisfactory terms with Myer on the subject of rent. In May 1879, it was announced that the property would pass into the possession of the Methodist Episcopal Conference, with the new title of Ashland College and Normal School (ACNS). Money to pay off the $3,700 debt was raised by public subscription, and in August, Myer sold the property to the trustees of the Methodist Episcopal Church for $3,700.

The quarterly Conference of the Church put management of ACNS in the trustees' hands. Reverend Lowell L. Rogers was the newly elected president of the Institution. Rogers was a Methodist minister from New York. He had been teaching, he said, for twenty-four years, beginning at age sixteen. He had taught at Willamette University the year prior to coming to Ashland and had been minister of the Methodist Church in Yreka. His contract with the trustees specified that he was to take charge of the School, nominate his own assistants, pay all expenses, and "make what he could of it." Tuition was to be the only source of revenue.

Rogers chose as his vice president Washington Irving Nichols, also originally a New Yorker, who graduated in 1862 from Genesee College (later Syracuse University). Nichols taught in Siskiyou County from 1869 to 1879. These two men and their wives formed the faculty of ACNS. Rogers was professor of moral and mental science. Nichols was professor of mathematics. Mrs. Rogers was the preceptress (in charge of the women students) and taught English grammar, while Mrs. Nichols taught music and French. It was added that "other competent instructors will be secured as fast as the needs of the institution require."

Hopes ran high. Courses of study were laid out for a six-year classical program (including preparatory studies), ending in bachelor's and master's degrees; a three-year scientific program with a BS degree; and diploma programs of three years each in normal, commercial, and musical studies. Tuition was $6 per month, rooms or cottages for "self-boarding" were listed at $2 to $5 per month, and board either in the College Boarding Hall or with private families cost between $3.50 and $4.50 per week. Ashland was advertised as a town with no saloons, where liquor was prohibited. The College was billed as being "under the supervision of an Evangelical Christian Church" but not "sectarian" in any "objectionable sense." Plans were afoot to raise an endowment of $250,000 so tuition could be reduced.

But things did not go well. There was a plaintive note in the papers in July 1879 asking subscribers to the College fund to pay up. Rogers said no one would be refused for whom a class of ten could be formed, and in the "higher departments," even that number would not be necessary. In November, it was said that there were 115 names on the student rolls, but two months later (January 1880), only 26 students were reported. The second figure is probably a count of the college-level students only, while the first figure represents the overall enrollment, including the primary grades. Indeed, the biennial reports sent to the state superintendent of public instruction gave an overall enrollment figure of 117 for 1880 and 148 for 1882, of which about 25 to 30 seem to have been college-level students. Perhaps the best indication of what was going on is that Rev. Rogers's salary dropped from $1,500 in 1880 to $1,200 in 1882.

In June 1880, Professor Nichols and his wife resigned and moved to Yreka, where he practiced law. The Board of Trustees elected LaDru Royal of Corvallis as professor of languages, Kate Thornton of Ashland as assistant teacher, and Ella Scott of San Francisco as teacher of vocal and instrumental music. In May 1881, three graduates received the first diplomas of the Ashland College and Normal School. The following month, the trustees elected LaDru Royal vice president of the College and professor of natural sciences. President

Rogers's wife, Ada, was appointed preceptress at a salary of $800. The president received $1,200; Mr. Royal, $1,000; and a new music teacher, Della Webber, earned $600. This raises some interesting questions about the Institution's finances. In the 1882 report to the state superintendent, the total income of the College is listed at $2,200, all from tuition. The salaries and other expenditures totaled $3,800. Something was wrong, and it is not surprising that at the beginning of the 1881–82 school year, the trustees appointed one of their own, Mr. Chapman, to serve as an "endowment agent" to raise money for the College.

In early 1882, signs of change became apparent. President Rogers indicated to the Board of Trustees in February that he intended to resign by the end of the school year due to poor health. At that same meeting, LaDru Royal requested leave for the spring term, also for health reasons. Expecting Royal's return, the trustees elected him president at their June meeting "for the ensuing year." But Royal went East for treatment and never returned to take office. In September 1882, the Methodist Church Conference announced the appointment of Miller G. Royal, LaDru's cousin, as the new president of the Ashland College and Normal School.

Miller Royal received his early education at the Umpqua Academy, where his father, Thomas Royal, was principal from 1859 to 1867. Miller graduated in 1864 and took his AB and AM degrees at Willamette University. He was twenty-eight years old when he assumed the presidency of the Ashland College and Normal School. On October 6, 1882, Royal's twenty-ninth birthday, the state legislature passed a bill creating state normal schools in Ashland and Monmouth. The governor reportedly signed the bill on November 3, 1882, and Ashland College and Normal School (ACNS) became an official state normal school. No financial support came with the title, however, and control remained with the Methodist Episcopal Church.

The College offered three courses of study: a college preparatory course, a commercial course, and the state normal course. Tuition ranged from four to twelve dollars per term, depending on the studies chosen, and board in the College Boarding Hall or with private families cost three or four dollars per week, depending on whether the student wanted food over the weekend. In fall 1883, it was said that attendance was "much larger than last year," but no supporting figures are available. The 1882 report to the state superintendent listed 148 students, while the 1884 report listed 142 students. In 1884, the *Tidings* complained that "upstate" papers (the *Oregonian* is mentioned by name) "studiously ignore the fact that there is a State Normal School in Ashland." Apparently, ACNS was headed downhill from the outset.

In January 1885, the governor proclaimed that the state's two normal schools "are in a flourishing condition." This elicited the comment from the *Tidings* that "while the schools are doing as well as can be expected under the circumstances, they should have financial aid rather than just the complimentary loan of the state's name."

The following October, there were about eighty students enrolled at the normal school. A year later (October 1886), the *Tidings* reported that "the ACNS has been closed since Prof. Royal resigned. The trustees do not intend to reopen. It will be offered to the state if the Methodist Episcopal Conference forfeits it by not maintaining a six-month term. The debt is $1,090."

When W. C. Myer sold the property to the Conference in 1879, it was with the proviso that at least a six-month term would be held every year; otherwise, the property would revert to Myer. Well, it did revert. The trustees decided not to reopen the Institution. Miller

Royal accepted the presidency of the normal school in Weston (near Pendleton), Oregon, and in November 1886, a Mrs. J. D. Crocker was "teaching a private school" in the college building. But the citizens of Ashland would not settle for that.

By June 1887, funds were being raised once again. Stockholders met and elected a board of regents, chose a new name—Ashland State Normal School (ASNS)—and appointed a committee to obtain the title to the ASNS property, which they did for $1,150. Meanwhile, the board elected professor J. S. Sweet, principal of the Ashland schools for the previous three years, as president. ASNS retained its designation as a state normal school. The regents established a "training school" and added a business department as well as special courses in art and music. ASNS offered a two-year Elementary Course, which included practice in the training school; a three-year Academic Course; and a four-year Advanced Course (thirty-six weeks each), which included teaching experience and culminated in a bachelor's degree in Scientific Didactics, conferring the right to teach in any school in the state.

ASNS lasted three years, with six students graduating in May 1890. But when the Ashland School District decided to develop its own high school, ASNS seems to have folded. In August 1890, Professor Sweet left Ashland to teach in Santa Rosa, California, and the Ashland School District leased part of the normal school building for $100 per year, apparently placing high school and some grammar school students in the building.

Once more, Ashland was without a college. This time, three years passed before there was any activity on that front. In order to understand that activity, we must switch our focus to the northern part of the state.

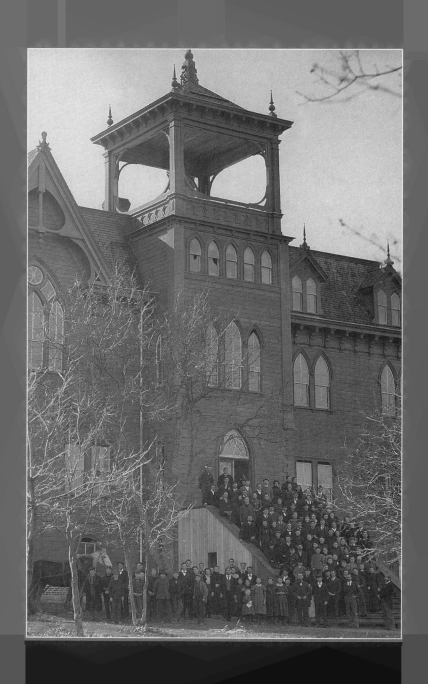

THE SECOND
INCARNATION

IN 1891, TWO LEADING administrators of Willamette University, President Thomas Van Scoy and Dean Charles C. Stratton, resigned and moved to Portland to found Portland University (PU), a Methodist institution. There, the two men swapped positions, Stratton becoming president and Van Scoy dean. PU was founded not with a cash endowment, but as part of a real estate development plan that allowed people to buy nearby lots. In the beginning, the plan was so successful that PU was soon worth about one million dollars. Plans were put forward to create branches based on the PU model throughout the Northwest.

Consequently, Ashland's Methodist minister, the Reverend Julius S. Smith, suggested creating such a branch in Ashland. In April 1893, Stratton, Van Scoy, and the financial agent, Reverend A. C. Fairchild, met with interested citizens at Ashland City Hall. The Portlanders estimated that the proposed institution would attract around 200 students from outside the community, with each student spending at least $200 for living expenses, totalling $40,000 a year for Ashland.

To bring about this happy state of affairs, the Portland University administrators wanted land and a $12,000 bonus in cash from the Ashlanders—a tract large enough to be developed and sold as building lots, and enough cash to begin construction of buildings for the new college. PU pledged to set up $20,000 worth of buildings once this bonus was raised. A governing board of trustees under the Methodist Episcopal Church's jurisdiction would be established, with seven members from Portland and seven from Ashland. Fall 1893 was the target date set for the opening of the Institution.

Ashland bought the proposal wholeheartedly. Several tracts of land were offered almost immediately, and by July 1893, leading citizens incorporated the Ashland Collegiate Institute (ACI), with Reverend Julius Smith designated as business manager and chief executive of the Institution. H. B. Carter transferred a tract of land (116 acres), known as the Bellview Tract, to the corporation for $12,000 at 8-percent interest annually for two years, and at 10 percent thereafter. Three lots were set aside for the Collegiate Institute, while the remaining land would be sold for real estate development at "not less than $200 per acre." Enthusiasm was high, construction began, and the debacle of 1869 was repeated when the financial panic of 1893 forced Portland University—which suddenly had to think of saving itself—to withdraw its commitment.

In January 1894, the *Tidings* reported that the "handsome new building" was sitting there with much of the exterior work done but otherwise unfinished. In short, it was a shell. However, local funding was still coming in, and this money must have been used for the purchase of Lots 1, 2, and 3 of the Bellview Tract, about a mile south of the present campus, at $1,500 for the Ashland Collegiate Institute. That accounted for about five acres of the original tract. The remainder presumably reverted to the original owner.

Old Southern Oregon Normal School

In early February 1895, G.W. Dunn, the local representative in the state legislature, introduced a bill to establish a state normal school in Ashland. The bill passed in the House, but the legislature adjourned without the necessary Senate action.

Once more, the citizens of Ashland rose to the challenge of salvaging the Institution. In June 1895, interested citizens met repeatedly, resulting in a series of interrelated deals whereby W.C. Myer (the legal owner of the old Academy property, which was now being used as the high school) sold Lots 1 and 2 in Block 7 to the Ashland School District for $1. In turn, the school district voted to buy the old normal school property for $3,000, which sum was then used by the old Ashland College and Normal School Association to take over the Ashland Collegiate Institute property, pay off its debts, and open the Institute in September under the control and charter of the old

Above: Southern Oregon State Normal School. Below: SOSNS faculty, with William Thomas Van Scoy.

group, but with a new name: Southern Oregon State Normal School (SOSNS).

The leader this new institution was William Thomas Van Scoy, a cousin of the Thomas Van Scoy who had been president of Willamette University. W. T. Van Scoy was an experienced educator and administrator. Born in Virginia in 1848, he later migrated West, obtained a degree from Northwestern University, headed the Sheridan Academy and the Jefferson Institute, and served as president of the state normal school in Drain, Oregon, from 1891 to 1894.

He was enthusiastic about a normal school in Ashland, and the board—now called regents—settled an agreement with him under which they were to finish and furnish the College buildings, and he was to run the College at his own expense.

School opened in September 1895 on a seven-and-a-half-acre campus with a newly built academic building and a dormitory for women. President Van Scoy was listed as professor of languages, psychology, and educational methods. In addition, he hired seven faculty members who were to handle

William Thomas Van Scoy

mathematics, natural sciences, history and geography, literature and elocution, bookkeeping and commercial law, instrumental and vocal music, and painting. Of these instructors, all but one was gone within four years. The one who stayed deserves special mention. He was Irving Vining, teacher of literature and elocution, who will reappear several times in these pages. (It was my melancholy duty to assess and dispose of Vining's personal library upon his death in Ashland in 1949.)

In 1895, SOSNS offered normal, academic, business, and advanced (for students planning to attend a university) programs. In addition, there were courses in music and art, and a model school was organized for the teacher-training program. Tuition, books, board, and lodging were advertised as available for $125 per year. The enrollment for that year was 133, not counting the model school. At that time, Ashland's population was not much more than 2,000.

A tradition-setting event occurred on Friday, March 20, 1896, when all students and faculty turned out during the first Campus Day to work on the grounds. Campus Day became an annual event thereafter, lasting into the 1980s. On this day, classes would be dismissed, and all of the faculty and students would help beautify the campus.

On June 11, thirty students graduated, twenty-three in the normal program, five in business (or commercial, as it was called), and two in academic programs. A summer school followed, in which twenty-one students completed review work in some dozen subjects ranging from Latin to orthography. One of the graduates of the 1896 class was Susanne Homes of Ashland, who would later become the county superintendent of schools and after whom the first women's dormitory of the new Institution (post-1926) was to be named.

The 1896–97 school year repeated the prior year's curriculum, except that the School added German, French, and Latin courses. It is worth noting at this point that, while the Institution officially called itself the Southern Oregon State Normal School, the board continued to use the old incorporated title of Ashland State Normal School. The newspapers of the time further compounded the confusion, using SOSNS in some articles and ASNS in others.

Enrollees of the Training School, 1907–1908

With the Spanish-American War underway, the School organized a cadet company under Vining's leadership toward the end of the 1897–98 academic year. That same year, Vining was in charge of the training school, in addition to teaching history and elocution. Obviously, it was a time when instructors were able to move rather easily from one subject area to another. In fall 1898, Instructor of Natural Sciences Rice Eubank resigned from SOSNS and accepted a position as a teacher of Greek and Latin at the University of Minnesota. At the same time, Fred Ulen, a graduate of the School's Commercial Department, accepted a position as an instructor in bookkeeping, also at the University of Minnesota. This speaks well of the quality of the instruction in Ashland during this period.

The 1898–99 academic year was a watershed period. E. V. Carter of Ashland, Speaker of the House in the Oregon state legislature, submitted a bill providing $15,000 for SOSNS—on the condition that a board of regents (to be appointed) receive a deed for the property, thus making the School a state institution in fact as well as in name.

The bill was entered in October 1898 and forwarded for the regular session of the legislature, which began in January 1899. Meanwhile, in December, the Ways and Means Committee of the legislature visited the Normal School. As many as 183 students were enrolled at the time. A member of the committee, Senator B. F. Mulkey, who was a faculty member at Monmouth normal school, spoke briefly to the assembled students and faculty. He must have made a good impression, because four years later, he was invited back as president of the Institution.

At the same time, culture was not neglected. While Carter's bill moved through the House, a well-known Shakespearean, Samuel Wells, presented *Hamlet*, *The Merchant of Venice*, and *Othello* in Ashland on January 30, 31, and February 1, with the proceeds going to the Normal School. The point is worth making, simply to demonstrate that Ashland's love for and engagement with Shakespeare dates back to the nineteenth century and was not a new development in 1935, as some have thought.

In mid-February, the Senate passed the normal school bill, although funding had been cut in half to $7,500. The bill provided for a board of regents comprising the governor, the secretary of state, the superintendent of public instruction, and nine additional persons to be appointed by the governor and approved by the Senate. In trust for the state of Oregon, the regents were to receive a deed for the property from the Ashland State Normal School Association for normal school purposes.

The promise of funding prompted plans for a variety of improvements. It was said that by September, a telephone line would be installed and electric lights provided. This gives some indication of the pioneer conditions under which the Institution had existed. Indeed, a complete sewer system was still seven years away. There was talk of building a street railroad on Siskiyou Boulevard between downtown and the Normal School, but there is no evidence that anything ever came of this. A men's dormitory was built during the summer "as a private investment by a progressive citizen." That building had two stories, with rooms for the training school classes downstairs and the dormitory upstairs.

The regents met in late April and received the titles to Lots 1, 2, and 3 of the Bellview Tract (the SOSNS property). There was a $1,500 encumbrance on the property, however, and the regents refused to accept it until the encumbrance was cleared. Again, the people of Ashland came to the rescue. They contributed $2,000 in two days. By mid-May, SOSNS was a full-fledged, state-supported institution.

At their June meeting, the regents retained W. T. Van Scoy as president and appointed the rest of the faculty to what were now called "chairs" of literature, science, and mathematics. In 1899, the regents appointed Alice Applegate as critic teacher and principal of the training school. She stayed for two years in this position, later marrying Emil Piel of Ashland and remaining in the community for many years. The president's salary was set at $1,100 for the year, plus $150 for travel. Two male professors were awarded $850 and $800, and at least four female professors received $650 each. These were probably ten-month contracts, for Applegate later noted that she was paid $65 per month. No salaries were allotted for the Music Department, since it was not a part of the Normal School's program, although several separate courses were included. Several weeks later, the mathematics professor, Mr. Talkington, resigned, and the regents hired W. M. Clayton of Ohio to take his place.

The 1899–1900 year began with an advertisement that listed tuition as $6.25 per term and lodging as $0.50 per week, with students furnishing their own "bed clothing." Board at the Normal School hall cost $1.75 per week, as opposed to between $2.50 and $3.00 with families in Ashland. It was still said that $125 paid all expenses for one year, including books. This was the year the state took control of the Institution. Construction of the men's dormitory was completed. Records show an enrollment of 202 students, down from 205 the previous year.

Perhaps the year's most noteworthy event was the promulgation of a rule that all athletes had to keep their grades up to at least the 80-percent level or be barred from participation. The first-year curriculum included algebra, grammar and rhetoric, physical geography, civil government, ancient history, reading, and drawing. The second year included plane geometry, English literature, medieval history, astronomy, zoology, physics, and vocal music. In the third year, students took solid geometry or Latin, psychology, English literature, ethics, geology, botany, and methods, along with American literature and current events. The fourth year included chemistry, history and philosophy of education, review of anatomy and physiology, methods and training, bookkeeping, political economy, constitution of Oregon, and Oregon school law. This curriculum was not markedly different from what it had been ten years earlier, or would become ten years later.

THE EARLY
TWENTIETH CENTURY

THE MOST STARTLING EVENT of 1900 occurred at the June meeting of the Board of Regents. When the board chose faculty for the following academic year, they elected W. M. Clayton—the newcomer from Ohio—president of the Institution, letting Van Scoy go. What precipitated this decision is now lost in history. Clearly, Van Scoy had seriously offended someone or been judged inadequate. A month later, Van Scoy became the principal of the Jacksonville schools.

The excitement over the presidential change was apparently so great that it was not until November, when the 1900–01 year was well underway, that the newspaper finally noted any other decisions made by the regents at their June meeting. The regents dropped the Business Department and all special studies, since the state had agreed to fund only the programs and courses related to the normal school function when it took over the Institution. The 1901 legislature appropriated $12,500 to SOSNS for two years, beginning January 1, 1901. This was a considerable improvement over the 1899 allocation of $7,500, and everyone seems to have been content with both the financing and the enrollment (205 students).

Clayton was reappointed president in 1901–02. His wife, Ardinell, served as the drawing teacher during his tenure. Enrollment was 206, and the year was a quiet one. Quiet, that is, until the end of the year. When the regents met in June 1902, they faced several interesting developments. Irving Vining, the last remaining member of the founding faculty, had resigned after seven years of service. He went East to study at Columbia University and the American Academy of

Dramatic Art, remaining in New York for a number of years. He later returned to Ashland, where he built the Vining Theatre in 1914, which he operated until 1925. Vining was a very popular lecturer and was invited to speak all over the state. From 1924 to 1928, he served as president of the Oregon State Chamber of Commerce.

Irving Vining (fourth from left, front row) as Shylock in an 1894 production of The Merchant of Venice

President Clayton also resigned, deciding to leave Ashland. In his stead, the regents elected Benjamin F. Mulkey, a forty-year-old faculty member of the Monmouth normal school, to the School presidency.

Born in Illinois in 1862, Mulkey arrived in Oregon with his parents in 1872. His father was a farmer at Pleasant Hill, near Eugene. Mulkey graduated from Monmouth in 1887. He taught school for five years before serving as the county clerk of Polk County from 1892–96. Mulkey was elected state senator from Polk County in 1896 and served in the legislature until 1901. He was later reelected from Jackson County and served until 1904. In 1897, Mulkey was appointed to the faculty at Monmouth. When Monmouth's president (Campbell) accepted the presidency at the University of Oregon, the students at Monmouth wanted Mulkey to assume the presidency there. A University of Oregon faculty member was brought in as president at Monmouth, however, and Mulkey came to Ashland. A completely new set of faculty members was hired, except for Esther Silsby, who taught music and whose name appears variously in the records, sometimes with her first name as "Ethel" or her last name as "Silsbee." She had begun teaching at SOSNS in 1899 and continued until the doors closed in 1909. One of the "new" faculty members was W. T. Van Scoy, who returned to the Institution—after two years of exile—as the professor of English and civics.

In 1902–03, enrollment shot up to 270 students, and training school enrollment had to be closed at 76. The Institution had so many people commuting to it that transportation between the city and the School became inadequate. It was reported that on one rainy morning in late September, fifty-six people gathered at Winter's Corner (Pioneer and Main), waiting for a horse-drawn bus that could not accommodate them all. SOSNS was now the largest normal school in the state, prompting the development of a strong athletic program. The School shaped up the grounds for football and engaged a coach, W. B. Scott, who had been the quarterback for the University of Oregon football team in 1900. The season's games present an interesting mélange. Although SOSNS lost to the University of Oregon (24–0) and Albany College (30–0), it defeated Roseburg High School (15–0) and Central Point (5–0).

Benjamin F. Mulkey

In January 1903, President Mulkey departed to serve in the legislature, and William Miller, the superintendent of schools of Lane County, filled his position temporarily. The legislature was kind to SOSNS in 1903, appropriating $18,836 for operating expenses for two years, plus an additional $8,000 for a new academic building. Senator Mulkey returned to his presidency at the end of February to a round of applause. In July, the senior class of 1903 published an annual, and President Mulkey sent copies to friends of the Institution. Entitled *Lamron Dnalhsa* ("Ashland Normal" spelled backward), the yearbook offered a fascinating snapshot of the Institution and its people.

That April, Shakespeare returned to town. Charles Hanford and Company presented *The Taming of the Shrew* at the Opera House, which stood on Main Street and Pioneer. Oscar Winter's grocery store was on the ground floor.

In June, the Board of Regents authorized the use of the $8,000 provided by the legislature for an additional academic building. That year, tuition receipts came to $2,523, which was a substantial increase over the previous year's $1,215.

Clyde Payne

The 1903–04 academic year was a banner year in every way, with most faculty continuing on. One new addition was Clyde Payne, who taught the natural sciences, bringing the total number of faculty members to eleven. The average salary was $890 per year, a considerable improvement; prior to state funding—when tuition provided the only income—faculty had been paid only $200 per year. Faculty typically taught seven classes daily, with forty-minute class periods.

In December, the new building was finished and accepted. Called the Administration Building, it had an eighty-six-foot frontage and a tower. The building was fifty-six feet deep and two stories high. On the first floor, to the right of the entrance, there was a teacher's study room. On the left were reception rooms for the public and students, plus a private office for the president. Behind the reception rooms was a library. At the rear, there were rooms for biology and chemistry on the left and a large classroom on the right. The laboratory rooms for the sciences were said to be "well equipped." The library held 1,500 volumes, and 2,500 volumes were available to students at the Ashland Public Library. A corridor ran through the building, leading to a thirty-eight-foot by fifty-foot gymnasium with connected dressing rooms, physical culture rooms, and showers. Upstairs were three classrooms on the left and two on the right, separated by sliding partitions that allowed the space to be used as an auditorium.

The old building became the training school, housing nine grades and a kindergarten. There were also facilities for manual training and school gardening. Together, the two academic buildings contained twenty-three rooms. The two dormitories (one for each gender) held sixty students apiece and were full. The campus boasted tennis courts, a running track, and playing fields for football and baseball. In addition to its football team, SOSNS now fielded both men's and women's basketball teams, as well as baseball and track teams.

Tuition remained nominal: $6.25 per term, or $25 per year for four terms of ten weeks each. A furnished room cost $0.50 per week, and board in the dining hall was $2.25 per week. Board with private families varied between $3 and $4 per week. Enrollment hit a high of 283 students, with tuition bringing in $2,900. There were more than 100 students in the training school. Students in the normal school program came from nineteen counties throughout Oregon, plus six students from California and five from Washington.

At their June 1904 meeting, the regents added an advanced course to the curriculum for the preparation of high school teachers.

The results of the interclass track meet, held in April 1905, give some idea of the physical standards of the time. Bert Stancliff won the 220-yard dash in 26 seconds. In the 440-yard run, the winning time was 59 seconds. The mile-run winner came in at 5 minutes, 18.4 seconds. The winner of the 120-yard hurdles took 17.4 seconds, and the fastest in the 220-yard hurdles was reported at 72 seconds (one must conclude that the 120 were high hurdles, and the 220

THIS PAGE
Above: Dormitory residents, 1904
Below: Old Southern Oregon Normal School

FACING PAGE
Above: SONS campus circa 1903, with
the new Administration Building
Below left: Ethel Osburn and Edna Kingkade
in Women's Dormitory, October 4, 1904
Below right, first row: Clare Sherwood,
Worth Harvey, Julia Olson, Almeda Cooper
Second row: Ida Robertson, Ernest Wright,
Carl Murphy, Edna Kingkade, Clarence
Burke

low, which was then standard practice). The best high jump was 4 feet, 11 inches, and the broad jump 18 feet, 10 inches. The shot put was 33 feet, 3 inches, and the hammer thrown 110 feet, 2 inches.

During the 1904–05 academic year, things took a downturn. Enrollment fell to 222. Next, a referendum petition in May 1905 cut off all funding for the state institutions until a vote could be held on the matter in June 1906. Suddenly, things looked pretty bleak, and in June 1905, the regents had to appoint teachers to carry on instruction while waiting for state and private funding.

Immediately, the community came forward. The Ashland Board of Trade (an early form of the Chamber of Commerce) said it would try to raise money for SOSNS. The faculty offered to go on half-pay. President Mulkey said $5,000 to $6,000 would see the School through. Ashland's two banks, the Bank of Ashland and the First National Bank of Ashland, announced they were putting up $500 each and would advance the remaining $5,000 (at 6-percent interest) if enough collateral could be raised by citizens of the community.

The citizens of Ashland came to the rescue again and provided the needed financial aid so the Institution could function for the 1905–06 year. Enrollment dipped to 207, although the 1906 graduating class was the largest ever, numbering 35. At the statewide election in June, the general appropriation bill was approved by a substantial majority, and all seemed to be well again. Ashland extended its water system out to the Institution. SOSNS invited bids for a heating plant and made additions to the laboratories and the library. There were plans to hire more faculty, and a year was added to the course of study. This last may or may not have been a real addition. It looks as though the School went from a three-year program of four terms per year to a four-year program of three terms per year—which then made possible the addition of a summer school program.

SOSNS football team, 1904

The 1906–07 academic year slid by with no great crises. The football team enjoyed an undefeated season for the first time. As expected, a summer school session was held, and attendees who wished to do so were invited to tent in the groves on campus for the session. Toward the end of the regular academic year, work began on the installation of a complete sewer system for the campus.

In July 1907, the governor named a single board of regents for all of the state's normal schools, and that board decreed a four-year curriculum for the state institutions. Having already met the new requirements, Southern Oregon State Normal School installed a new manual training program for teachers. The School set up twelve workbenches, complete with tools, to accommodate twenty-four students. H.H. Wardripp from San Jose, California, was hired to run the program, at an annual salary of $1,000.

The 1907–08 year began with some good news for students: tuition was canceled! An "incidental fee" of $12, however, was levied. This amounted to $6 per semester, and that is the first indication that a move had been made from the quarter system to a semester system. That year, there were fifteen instructors on the faculty.

But there was political trouble brewing in the state. Many felt Oregon could not afford to support its educational institutions as they were then constituted. Accomplished politician that he was, Mulkey no doubt sensed this, and, despite his raise, chose to get out. He resigned at the end of December 1907, accepting a partnership in the Jackson County Abstract Company with the intention of practicing law (he was an attorney) and handling the company's court business in Jacksonville. Before 1908 was out, he had been elected district attorney of Jackson County.

Meanwhile, the regents selected Clyde Payne to serve as acting president for the remainder of the academic year. Shortly thereafter,

Clyde Payne (third from right)

the governor appointed a special committee of three to inspect and report on the state's normal schools, which were located in Ashland, Drain, Monmouth, and Weston. The appropriation bill for the normal schools passed by the 1907 legislature contained a provision for the appointment of an inspection committee. The members of the committee, as appointed by the governor, were all superintendents of schools in their respective cities: J. M. Powers of Salem, J. A. Churchill of Baker, and R. R. Turner of Grants Pass. Churchill would appear again almost two decades later as president of the next incarnation of the Normal School.

The Normal School inspectors visited SOSNS in late April 1908. After spending two days on campus talking with students and faculty and carefully examining all facets of the Institution, they reported to the governor that the institutions were underfunded and lacked adequate equipment and supplies.

When the Board of Regents met in Salem on July 2, the regents debated how many normal schools could be funded. Two board members supported all four of the existing institutions, and four members wished to cut the institutions down to two (not indicating which two). In the end, they compromised on a vote of five to four to retain three normal schools. The normal school at Drain was abandoned.

The regents then elected Harry Shafer, president of the normal school at Cheney, Washington, as the new president of Southern Oregon State Normal School. Shafer was a graduate of Eureka College in Illinois (later known as the alma mater of former president Ronald Reagan). Shafer earned bachelor's and master's degrees at Harvard and attended Teachers' College of

Harry Shafer

Columbia University. He headed the Education Department in the State Normal School at San Diego before attending Cheney. He was a well-prepared, respected educator. Unfortunately, normal school education in Oregon had become a lost cause by the time he arrived.

In February 1909, the legislature adjourned without appropriating funds for the normal schools. A special session was called in March to deal with the problem. While the house passed a funding bill, the senate refused to go along. Once more, the local citizens rushed into the breach. They organized a committee to raise funds, and they cooperated with the regents by furnishing security for monies advanced through the state treasurer for expenses. By mid-April, the committee reported that about half the necessary funds had been raised. In May, however, the regents decided to close all of the normal schools at year's end, placing SOSNS in the hands of a custodian, W.M. McIntire, and leaving final disposition to the legislature.

At the end of May, the junior class of SOSNS published an annual, the *Chrysanthemum*. It contained pleas for the preservation of the School, but to no avail. In June, President Shafer accepted the position of vice-chancellor of Pennsylvania State University, and most of the remaining faculty took jobs elsewhere.

W.T. Van Scoy organized and was president of the College Preparatory and Business School that opened in September 1909 in Ashland, but it was short-lived. We find him as a teacher at the new Ashland High School in 1911–12. He fell on hard times in his last years, and former students and friends raised funds to help him. He died in Rogue River in 1918.

Meanwhile, what had once been SOSNS sat and rotted. Much of the equipment was disposed of as state property. Typical of the sort of bureaucratic actions that transpired is the fate of the horse-drawn bus that carried students from town to campus; it was sold to someone in Salem for forty dollars. Thereafter, the state shipped it to Salem, at a cost of sixty-seven dollars! This occurred in January 1910.

The Normal School bus

In July 1910, an initiative petition was submitted that would have provided for the support and maintenance of SOSNS, Monmouth, and Weston. But in the general election in November, Monmouth alone was successful. Ashland lost by more than 10,000 votes. Most of the voters were upstate, and while willing to support an institution in their own region, they obviously were not willing to pay for institutions in the east and the south.

B. F. Mulkey (right)

The 1911 legislature met and ended with no further mention of reviving SOSNS, although they did provide $7,000 to settle the School's debts contracted in 1909, mostly for salaries. The property remained in state control until 1937, when the State Board of Higher Education sold it (Lots 1, 2, and 3 of the Bellview Tract) to Lottie Beswick of Ashland for $2,500.

But the local community never quit trying. In January 1914, citizens of Ashland launched a campaign to reestablish SOSNS. This ultimately resulted in a huge meeting on September 28, attracting 3,000 people. Schools let out, and all stores closed that afternoon. B. F. Mulkey spoke on the benefits of normal schools. Citizens contributed more than $3,000 to the Normal School Fund. The object was to convince voters to pass the initiative for the schools that had been placed on the statewide ballot for the November general election. A letter-writing campaign was undertaken. On November 5, 1914, a

The 1926–27 SOSNS faculty. Front row: Margaret Cason, Lillian Nicholson, Marion Elizabeth Wilson, Clara Augusta Trotter. Second row: Verne V. Caldwell, Pearl Durst, Eva Laura White, Georgia Mooney, Elizabeth Cook Richardson, Martha Isabella Wattenbarger, Beatrice Hall, Edith Louise Bork. Third row: Wayne Winfield Wells, Bertha Aline Stephens, Virginia Hales, Marion Elizabeth Ady. Fourth row: Arthur Samuel Taylor, Arthur C. Strange, Mattie Elizabeth Hileman, Walter Redford, Katherine Marion Vincent, Helen C. Anderson, Leona G. Marsters, Julius Alonzo Churchill.

trial ballot in Ashland showed 1,661 "yes" votes and 69 "no" votes. But, alas, on November 9, the normal schools lost again, going down 86,964 to 109,295. This time, Lane and Multnomah Counties voted for the measure, along with the southern Oregon counties, but the "no" vote in Marion and Clackamas Counties was so large that it carried the day.

When the legislature met in 1915, the defeat at the recent general election was still fresh enough to discourage any attempts at revival. But at the next session, the representative from Jackson County, Ben Shelden, entered a measure to place the normal school issue on the general election ballot of 1918. In February 1917, both the house and the senate voted for the measure. Once again, a local committee was formed and a campaign begun that carried on through most of 1917 and 1918. Once again, the answer was "no." The bill went down by 16,135 votes. It was clear that a popular statewide vote was not the way to go. The legislature itself was the only real hope and, even there, the time would not be judged ripe for seven years.

In 1925, that time had come. George Dunn of Ashland was a prominent member of the state senate, and a bill prepared by local people was entered into legislative proceedings in early January. The bill called for $175,000 in construction funds and asked the community to provide the site. By now, it was obvious that the old site would not suffice, and so the way was cleared for a third incarnation of the Normal School. In late January, the Ashland delegation— which visited the key Ways and Means Committee of the legislature—pledged that Ashland would indeed donate a site, in addition to making its public schools available for practice teaching.

Julius Alonzo Churchill

Since a normal school for eastern Oregon was also included in the bill, the political forces lined up quite favorably. On February 20, the house passed the bill 47–9, and on February 24, the senate passed the bill with only three negative votes. On March 4, the governor signed the bill into law. Ashland would once more have an institution of higher education in its environs.

Within a month, the regents appointed Julius Alonzo Churchill president of the Southern Oregon State Normal School. Churchill was born in Ohio in 1863. He graduated from Ohio Northern University in 1883 with a degree in civil engineering, later earning a master's degree there, as well. He came West and entered education. Churchill was school principal in Baker, Oregon, in 1888

41

and became the superintendent of Baker public schools from 1891 to 1913. In 1913, the governor appointed Churchill the superintendent of public instruction for the state. He was reelected to that post in 1914, 1918, and 1922. Churchill was, of course, by virtue of his state position, a member of the Board of Regents at the time of his appointment, but that appointment was set to begin when his term ended. He was given a four-year contract starting January 1, 1926.

At the same time, the regents hired John Bennes of Portland as the architect for a new building, and they visited Ashland to select a suitable site. The regents met with a local committee and looked at various possible sites. By late May, they decided that the old normal school site was inadequate. It was too small and too far from town. Finally, they selected a site just beyond where the Ashland General Hospital stood at the time—ground now occupied by Stevenson Union.

The city of Ashland immediately obtained an option for the land (about twenty-four acres) and scheduled a vote for June 15 on a bond issue for $18,000 for "Normal School Site Bonds." The bond issue passed 844 to 15, and construction began. The building was to be completed within a year. Curiously, the building in Ashland (now known as Churchill Hall) has a virtual double in La Grande, where the Eastern Oregon Normal School (EONS) was erected in 1927, using the same architect and plans.

Ashland had kept its commitments. The third incarnation for higher education in Ashland was about to begin.

THE THIRD INCARNATION

THE STATE LEGISLATURE had appropriated $175,000 for the new normal school at Ashland in 1925. Of this sum, $146,448 went to the Administration Building itself, including heating, plumbing, wiring, and the architect's fee ($6,974). The amount of $5,000 went to developing the grounds, and another $5,000 was stipulated for library books, which were selected by Cornelia Marvin, secretary of the Oregon State Library.

Several emergencies arose during construction. A twenty-four-inch pipe had to be installed for drainage at a cost of $1,000, and wiring changes and water pressure reduction ran to hundreds of dollars more. All in all, about $17,000 remained to cover furnishings and contingencies.

At the same time, a new public school (to be called Lincoln School) was also being built in Ashland just two blocks away. The Board of Regents committed $20,000 toward the construction of Lincoln School, which would serve as a training school for Southern

Oregon State Normal School students. SOSNS chose the critic teachers, and the school district employed them, contributing no less than $100 per month for nine months toward their salaries, matched by SOSNS. The school district provided heat, light, and janitorial service. SOSNS managed and controlled this public school, but it abided by school district rules regarding attendance, length of the school day, and student conduct. The district school nurse was given visitation rights to Lincoln School at no cost to SOSNS, which was also given the right to use the other elementary schools in the district for teacher-training purposes.

J. A. Churchill, the Normal School president, was a man with a great deal of educational experience and firm ideas about how to organize and run a school. In 1926, he was sixty-three years old and had served in upper-level education positions in Oregon for thirty-eight years: three years as a school principal, twenty-two years as a city superintendent, and thirteen years as the state superintendent of public instruction. One of his strongest beliefs was that the president of an institution should run all aspects of the School and be held accountable by the Board of Regents. The board had committees on teachers, libraries, and the course of study, and the members had involved themselves in these matters in the past. In a communication to the board, Churchill declared that he should select the teachers (with the board electing them thereafter), rely on his librarian and faculty for textbook selections, and set the course of study. While there is no written record of the board's response to this, it is clear that they went along with his desires. He hired the faculty, ordered library materials, and set the course of study.

To begin with, Churchill established a school year comprising three quarters of twelve weeks each, with a summer session consisting of two six-week periods. He hired faculty on a twelve-month basis, except in Lincoln School, where nine-month contracts were the rule. Full-time faculty were not allowed to do any kind of work outside their academic work. Faculty were to have master's degrees, but exceptions were sometimes made for teachers with many years of experience. Faculty were to start at salaries of $2,800 for men and $2,400 for women. These salaries were to be increased $100 per year, with the maximum to be determined by the board. (Regarding the differential between men's and women's salaries, it was assumed that most men would be married and have families to support, while the women were single. Married women were not hired.) The training school teachers were to receive $1,800 for nine months (there was a minimum of $1,600) and annual $100 increases to a maximum of $2,000. The Ashland School Board paid half of their salaries.

By June 1926, President Churchill had hired twenty-two faculty members for the coming school year. Ten women were hired to staff the training school, and twelve were members of the Normal School faculty. Of these twelve, seven were women, including the librarian, Pearl Durst, and the registrar, Katherine Vincent. Churchill violated his own rules in the hiring of this faculty, both in the degree requirements and salaries. Of the twenty-two hired, only six had master's degrees.

The west end of the Administration Building housed the library. Cornelia Marvin of the State Library spent the $5,000 allotted her for books, purchasing about 3,500 volumes, plus some 75 periodicals. An additional 229 volumes came from the old normal school, which had been closed in 1909. The Ashland Public Library had held these books in the intervening years. The librarian was given a materials budget of $1,000 for the year. She quickly stated that this was not enough money and that she would need some assistants.

Churchill laid out the curriculum for this new two-year Normal School for elementary school teachers based on his conviction that the course of study "must more or less definitely be prescribed." He thought there should be some limited electives to provide for individual differences and specialization, but that the basic program had to present a sound general cultural background and "a mastery of professional principles and technique." For the cultural background, he specified work in English (including grammar, composition, and literature), science (including biology and physical science), social science (including general history, American history, sociology, economics, and geography), health and physical education, art, music, and library instruction. On the professional side, he listed the courses Introduction to Teaching, Principles of Primary and Intermediate Education, Psychology, Educational Tests and Measurements, and Practice Teaching.

Out of this curriculum came the School's required program, which consisted of 14 credits of English spread over five quarters, 9 credits of biology, 2 credits of physical science, 2 credits of sociology (called Organization of Society), 6 credits of geography, 3 credits of economics, 2 credits of American history, 3 credits of health education, 3 credits of physical education, 6 credits of art, 6 credits of music, and 2 credits of library methods, for a total of 58 credits. The professional courses included Introduction to Teaching (3 credits); Primary or Intermediate Methods (6 credits); Social Organization of the School (2 credits); Psychology (9 credits); School Organization (2 credits); History of Education (2 credits); Educational Tests and Measurements (2 credits); Principles of Education (3 credits); and Practice Teaching (9 credits), for a total of 38 credits of work in education. The overall total was 96 credits, made up of 16 credits per quarter for six quarters.

Obviously, this program was indeed "prescribed," and it is difficult to see where there was room for electives at all. Yet it is forward-looking in at least one way—requiring students to learn how to use the library. One would think this basic for any college student, yet most institutions have not discovered the idea of library instruction to this day. For the first two years, the library work was placed in the sixth quarter; thereafter, it was given in the first quarter where, after all, it makes the most sense. The title was changed to Library Instruction, and the course continued until 1937, when, sadly, it was dropped from the program.

With the building completed, the faculty in place, and the curriculum set, it was time for school to begin. On June 21, 1926, 173 students enrolled in summer session. Five days later, the Institution was formally dedicated. Dr. Henry Suzzallo, president of the University of Washington, gave the dedicatory address (for which he was paid $100). As many as 500 people attended a dinner at the Ashland Armory. This time, the Normal School was off to a rousing start.

Churchill was hoping for more than 173 students in the regular session, and in August he sent more than 3,000 personal letters to high school graduates in the region extolling the advantages of attending SOSNS. It must have had some affect, because 273 students enrolled for the fall term that first academic year.

These students paid six dollars per quarter for tuition, plus three dollars for a student body fee and one dollar for health, at a total of ten dollars. Room and board was available in the community for thirty-one dollars per month, and it was said that students who wished to provide their own food could rent light housekeeping rooms for as little as two dollars per week.

The students came to a campus consisting of one building with eighteen classrooms, a gymnasium, a library, administrative offices,

and a 600-seat auditorium. The building sat on a twenty-four-acre campus, four acres of which were across the boulevard on the north side. The main campus fronted on Siskyou Boulevard and was bounded by Palm Street, Indiana Street, and Madrone Street, with Ashland Street running through it (behind the Administration Building). The Ashland General Hospital was on the boulevard east of Palm Street, and the Normal School land was east of the hospital.

An entering student had to be a graduate of a standard, four-year high school "or its equivalent." Those claiming equivalency had their credentials examined by a faculty committee. Students were also expected to conform to high social and ethical standards of conduct.

With school underway, it was quickly decided that the campus needed a student newspaper and a basketball team. A contest was held to determine the paper's name. Chosen from thirty-three entries judged by a faculty and student committee, the *Siskiyou* was submitted by Alex Bowman—who won the one-dollar contest prize. As soon as the first *Siskiyou* was published, an interesting distinction in institutional nomenclature became apparent. The official name displayed on the catalogs was "Southern Oregon State Normal School." The *Siskiyou*, however, consistently printed "Southern Oregon Normal School" and referred to the Institution in short form as "SONS." The newspapers, especially the sportswriters, quickly picked this up.

President Churchill hired Walter Hughes as the basketball coach. Hughes had spent six years as the coach at Ashland High School and had produced one state championship team. SONS played seventeen games that season, winning ten of them. All of the home games were played at the Ashland Armory. As soon as the basketball season ended in March, Coach Hughes resigned, leaving for Denver to go into business.

Even though the School was only a few months into its existence, it was already clear that more facilities were needed. The Board of Regents favored adding a women's dormitory and a gymnasium. President Churchill convinced them to request only the women's dormitory, at a cost of $150,000. This request was officially submitted to the legislature, which passed the bill for the dormitory on February 25, 1927. Less than two weeks later, on March 11, Governor Patterson vetoed the dormitory bill on the grounds that there were insufficient funds for it in the budget. Lack of adequate funding was to be an old and recurring story in the history of the Institution.

Among the items worth mentioning during this first academic year: Alumni V. V. Caldwell and Arthur Taylor were awarded master's degrees from the University of Idaho and the University of Washington respectively, thus confirming Churchill's faith in them. Incidentally, Caldwell was a genuine war hero, having served for twenty-two months during World War I through five battles in France, Belgium, Luxembourg, and Germany. He was awarded two Croix de Guerre Medals and recommended for the Distinguished Service Cross.

Regent John Fuller was busy on behalf of the School. He explained that "he had salvaged a certain amount of material" from the old normal school, which was rotting away, and sold it for the benefit of the present school. He said that the old buildings were in decay and that legislative authority should be sought to dispose of them before they became worthless. That was to take ten more years. President Churchill said that the funds from the sale of Fuller's salvage material had been used toward the purchase of a new piano.

The 1927–28 academic year began well, with 345 students registered. This was a 26-percent increase, and Churchill was elated. He did not hesitate to report this to the Board of Regents. He also spent a good deal of time writing to all of the superintendents and

The junior class of 1927–1928

principals who were employing SOSNS graduates, asking for detailed information on their work, scholarship, personality, and character. He promised that the information provided would be confidential.

This request may horrify most present-day readers and raise the specter of lawsuits galore, but such requests were common practice at the time. As the president reported to the board, all those addressed responded, "usually in much detail." Churchill added that most of the reports were "highly gratifying," while "a few . . . indicated partial or complete failure." Of course, this was precisely what Churchill was after. He was trying to determine what might improve the Institution's mission. When he checked the student records of those with the negative reports, he concluded that their failure might have been predicted. As a result, Churchill placed new rules on the books. First, any student with less than a 3.0 grade point average (equivalent to a C) for the first year would be dropped from school because they would not qualify for Practice Teaching. Further, students who did not achieve at least a 3.0 grade in Practice Teaching would not graduate. He commented to the board that not all entering students were suitable for teaching, noting that "a normal school must meet its responsibility in eliminating a considerable percentage of its students each year." How times have changed! Churchill told the board that all entering students would be given a set of objective examinations in September that would cover IQ, mathematics, spelling, geography, and U.S. history, and that all deficiencies thus identified would be corrected prior to Practice Teaching. He was genuinely intent on producing well-prepared teachers for the state.

It was an exciting year at SOSNS. Roy McNeal had been hired as the new coach, and he quickly organized a football team. This was not an easy matter on a campus with fewer than sixty men. (Indeed, the *Siskiyou* claimed there was a great need for a men's-only organization, since men were such a minority on campus—a situation that would continue through World War II. Nevertheless, women voted men into most of the elective offices. Men served as presidents of the student body, as well as of the junior and senior classes.)

Football was played on the high school field, since there were no college athletic facilities available. The first scheduled game had to be called off due to an infantile paralysis epidemic. The game, which was later rescheduled, was against the Humboldt State Teachers. The season was a successful one when it finally got underway. Ashland won all of the games: Albany College (21–0), Humboldt State (30–0), and Monmouth Normal (19–12).

Basketball and football were by no means the only activities. There was a men's and women's rifle club (eighteen men, seventy-five women), as well as a riding club (thirty-two women). Horseback

The football season began with a tragedy. Popular quarterback Max Newson collapsed during practice on October 13 and died that evening. It cast a pall of sadness across the campus. Overall, it was not a very successful season, with one win, two ties, and three losses. The record in basketball was better. The Siskiyou Braves, or Roaring Redskins, won six of nine games, and T-Bone Caldwell had a banner year on the court. (Many years later, I had the privilege of working with T-Bone when he was superintendent of schools at Lakeview and I was just out of the Army.) That winter, SOSNS entered the California Coast Athletic Conference, which was made up of twelve normal schools and junior colleges. Also, the SOSNS athletic field was named Fuller Field, in honor of John Fuller for his many efforts on behalf of the Institution. Fuller had been the manager of the Ashland Chamber of Commerce and Ashland's postmaster. He was a key figure in the establishment of the School.

On February 9, 1929, a bill was entered into the state legislature to create a single state board of higher education that would replace the three Boards of Regents then in existence (one for the University in Eugene, one for the State College in Corvallis, and one for the three normal schools). The state had just opened its third normal school in LaGrande—built on the same model as the school at Ashland. Its first president was Harvey Inlow, a 1906 graduate of SOSNS. The bill passed and was signed into law by the governor on March 1, 1929. From this point on, SOSNS answered to the newly created Oregon State Board of Higher Education, comprising nine members appointed by the governor. One of the members was C.L. Starr of Portland, who had served on the normal school Board of Regents. Also serving on the state board was Albert Burch of Medford, a well-known mining engineer and the only representative of the Rogue Valley.

Several noteworthy events transpired during the spring 1929 term. First, it was determined that a large 'O' should be built on the side of Grizzly Peak prior to the first Campus Day, which was set for May 15. The day before, dozens of the men and many of the women turned out to build an 'O' out of whitewashed stone, which measured 200-feet high by 100-feet wide. On Campus Day, classes were cancelled and everyone—students and faculty together—spent time beautifying the campus.

A. C. Joy

In June, Irving Vining was the toastmaster at the third alumni banquet, where A. C. Joy—who had been a faculty member of the old SOSNS that had closed in 1909—presented the bell from the original building to the present school.

Beginning with the 1929–30 academic year, SOSNS became part of the Oregon State System of Higher Education (OSSHE) under a single board. (The Oregon State System comprised the degree-granting, publicly supported schools: originally the University in Eugene, the State College in Corvallis, and the three normal schools in Monmouth, Ashland, and LaGrande. Later, Portland State University and the Oregon Institute of Technology (OIT) in Klamath Falls were added. One board, the Oregon State Board of Higher Education, ran the Oregon State System. Board members were appointed by the governor, and they appointed a chancellor.) It took three years for the full effects of that change to become evident at SOSNS. But some differences were immediately apparent. While resident tuition was still eleven dollars per term, a six-dollar fee for nonresident students was added. The catalog for the year stated that the library now contained 4,000 volumes. Also, the required credit for Practice Teaching was increased from 9 to 15 credits.

The biggest news on the national scene was the collapse of the stock market, which led to years of depression. This may have been a factor in the enrollment drop. That term, only 300 students appeared—a 22-percent decrease from the previous year. But President Churchill made a virtue out of the decline. In his report to the state board, he pointed to the drop in enrollment as "something worthwhile." He added that a normal school should eliminate those who are not suitable for teaching, which "heightens the quality of our product." Why he thought those who didn't enroll would not have been suitable for teaching is anyone's guess. He went on, in several reports that year, to insist that this normal school was different in a number of ways. He pointed to the test given in basic subjects to all students, with the requirement that deficiencies be removed. He stated that there were fewer methods courses given at Ashland, because he viewed most such courses as "valueless." As a result, it was possible to require more work in basic subjects like English, biology, psychology, history, and geography.

In these early reports to the new state board, Churchill reiterated the salary policies that had been set in 1926. He emphasized again that SOSNS faculty salaries were twelve-month contracts, as opposed to the nine-month contracts elsewhere in the system, so a $2,400 salary was really only equal to $1,800 at SOSNS. Churchill declared that departments weren't needed in his school because everyone was directly responsible to the president. He also felt that faculty members should take a term off without pay every third year for rest, travel, or study. Given the admittedly low salaries, it is difficult to see how this could have been thought possible. Churchill also made the point that more travel funds were needed. He said that only one trip to an educational convention had been taken since 1926 (by him, to Spokane). He thought that he ought to go to a major education conference every year, and that instructors should be able to attend out-of-state conferences for their own professional growth.

He pointed out that his budget request for the next biennium was $1,000 less than it had been for the previous term, although there were several desperately needed building projects: the gymnasium ($200,000), the women's dormitory ($175,000), and an auditorium for the training school ($50,000).

During the fall 1929 term, the junior class painted the 'O' on Grizzly Peak under the leadership of Class President John Billings, with the women providing the food. There was also the start of a football rivalry with newly established Eastern Oregon State Normal School.

Harvey Edgar Inlow

It seems that Churchill was concerned about what might be done if the game with Eastern ended in a tie. Churchill was a small man, about five feet, six inches tall, and an avid golfer, while President Inlow was a big man, about six feet, two inches tall. On November 6, 1929, Churchill wrote to Inlow proposing that should the game end in a tie, the presidents could settle matters via a golf tournament. Inlow responded that as the challenged party, he was the one to choose the contest, and he proposed a wrestling bout!

As it turned out, it was not possible to schedule a game that year. The Siskiyous already had seven games scheduled, of which they lost four, tied one, and won two. The first game with Eastern took place in fall 1930, and Southern won 14–0.

There were two other newsworthy items that year. It was decided that a yearbook would be introduced, to be called the *Madrona*. And it was announced that the student loan fund, which had started in 1927 with a few hundred dollars contributed by faculty and students, now held $1,770, and that students could borrow up to $75 with no interest.

The city of Ashland continued to be highly supportive. Business in Ashland was suspended from 2 to 5 p.m. on Friday, November 15, for the SOSNS–Chico football game, which SOSNS won 20–7. And Ashland businessmen put up the money to meet the guarantee to Chico. In July, the City Council agreed to donate the stage scenery from the Chautauqua building to the School for use in its own programs.

The 1930–31 academic year saw enrollment drop again by almost 4 percent, but there were some pleasant signs on the academic side. Wayne Wells was awarded a PhD in biology from the University of Washington, making him the first faculty member to obtain a doctorate. The library collection had risen to 6,000 volumes, and the loan fund had reached $2,000.

The *Siskiyou* declared that School tradition consisted of painting the 'O' before the first football game of the season, on Homecoming Day, and on Campus Day. It also noted that the School colors, chosen by President Churchill, were vermilion and sand—a reflection of the fall colors in the bushes and grass on the side of Grizzly Peak. At the end of this football season (four games won and two lost), the football squad chose halfback Claude Hines of Baker, the first and only black student at the time, as honorary captain for the year.

In his report to the board on April 29, 1931, Churchill apparently felt he had to repeat all of the information he had included in his 1930 report. He emphasized once again that the faculty salaries at SOSNS were twelve-month salaries and that $2,800 at SOSNS would be only $2,100 at the nine-month institutions. He pointed out that one of his instructors was given a principalship at Grants Pass for $2,500.

There was a $500,000 budget cut set for the state system, and Southern's share of that was 1.6 percent, or $8,000. Some $1,834 of that was to come from capital outlay, $1,000 from the library, and $500 from supplies, leaving $4,600 to be cut. Churchill said he would either have to cut salaries by 5 percent or eliminate some function. He would agree to the salary cut, he said, only if it were to be done in all of the schools. As for function, he said the SOSNS had no function to cut. He told the board that he wanted to cooperate, but reminded them that their support had been "wholly inadequate." He quoted the Bible, writing, "'From him that hath not shall be taken away even that which he hath.' Need the biblical prophecy be fulfilled?" Churchill asked.

The upshot of it all came in Churchill's proposed budget for 1931–32, which he submitted on June 13, 1931. In this budget, spending came to $6,617 less than the expenditures for the previous budget. Faculty salaries were not cut at this point.

It was at about this time that Churchill stated in a letter to V.V. Caldwell, the instructor of psychology, that "the personality of a president should put its stamp on the institution." That had certainly been true of his administration.

In its June issue, the *Siskiyou* reported that seven former SOSNS students, now at the University of Oregon, had been elected to Phi Beta Kappa, the national honorary academic society. This speaks very well of the academic program at SOSNS.

Baseball team, 1931

In 1931, faculty member Arthur Taylor returned from leave wearing a mustache. This bothered President Churchill so much that he included a note on it in his papers, saying "he feels that Taylor hadn't taken his bath every time he comes into the office." He added, "The faculty feels the same." So strong was Churchill's power that it became "policy" for "everyone to look and laugh every time they see him." Taylor shaved off the mustache.

A new instructor was hired in English and dramatics who would later have a great impact on the Rogue Valley: Angus Bowmer.

The 1931–32 academic year brought several new developments. The president announced that SOSNS would now function as a junior college in addition to retaining its normal school responsibilities, according to the state board. Furthermore, Churchill decided to offer night classes for the benefit of "the citizens of the valley."

The night classes were a success, with work offered in sociology, speech, and geography. Enrollment jumped about 19 percent, and things were looking good. But the Great Depression was beginning to affect the region, and in November, the faculty pledged to give one day's salary out of each month for five months to aid the needy and unemployed. The other institutions in the state system did the same, at the request of Governor Meier, who was responding to President Hoover's request to governors. Later that term, in December, the faculty organized itself into a chapter of the American Association of University Professors (AAUP), with Wayne Wells as its president.

In 1932, the state board officially dropped the SOSNS designation for the Institution and moved to what had been used unofficially for

Walter Redford

some time: Southern Oregon Normal School, or SONS. It was a busy time. The presidency at Monmouth became vacant, and the state board appointed Churchill to that position, as well as making him director of all elementary school education in Oregon. From this point, the normal school presidents reported directly to him. Churchill left SONS on June 30, 1932, taking four of the faculty with him: Helen Anderson, Eloisa Buck, Vern Caldwell, and Clara Trotter. The state board appointed Walter Redford to assume the SONS presidency on July 1, 1932.

With Churchill's departure and the elevation of Redford to the presidency, Roy McNeal moved out of his coaching position and took over the instruction of geography, which had been Redford's teaching assignment. This left the coaching position open, and Howard Hobson, who had been the coach at Benson High School in Portland, was employed to fill that position. Under Hobson's coaching, the SONS basketball team repeatedly defeated the University of

Oregon's varsity team, and it is fair to offer a brief reprise of the Hobson career. He was at SONS for three years, and then, in 1935, he was appointed head coach for basketball at the University of Oregon, where he earned a national title and worked until 1947. In 1948, he became the coach at Yale University, retiring in 1956. His career was a distinguished one, and he is honored in the Basketball Hall of Fame for his achievements. His time at Southern Oregon Normal School was precious to his memory, as he stated in a visit to the campus shortly before his death in 1991.

Another new hire—worthy of mention for her long and distinguished service—was the new English instructor, Ollie Depew, from Kentucky. This was also the year station KMED produced the first SONS radio program, with Foss Kramer as the announcer and piano player. Angus Bowmer presented his first Shakespeare play, *As You Like It*, in modern dress, with both faculty and students in the cast.

It was during this time that the legislature placed the Zorn-MacPherson Bill before the voters, which was designed to eliminate the normal schools and make SONS a junior college. Of course, the community immediately organized a committee of outstanding citizens (G.M. Green, W.H. McNair, H.O. Enders, G.W. Dunn, Fred Homes, and John Fuller) to save SONS. A campaign went on throughout the fall, and the bill was soundly defeated in the November general election.

This was not the only problem. The state board was attempting to cope with a serious deficit of $160,000, and institutions were called on to help balance the budget. Three tactics were employed the following academic year: the faculty volunteered 5- to 15-percent salary reductions on a sliding scale, presidents reduced their budgets, and additional student fees were levied.

In the 1933–34 academic year, the president's salary dropped 23 percent, from $5,000 to $3,850. Male faculty suffered 17-percent decreases, and female faculty 15-percent decreases. These reduced salaries remained in effect for five years. It was 1938 before salaries returned to 1932 levels. At the same time, student tuition and fees increased from $11 per term to $14. This may not look like much of a jump, but it is a 27-percent increase. The state system budgets were also reduced, and the SONS budget, which had been $90,415 in 1932–33, was cut to $66,547 for 1933–34, a drop of more than 26 percent. Indeed, President Redford bemoaned the fact that there had been a 50-percent reduction in the state education budget from its high point in 1929–30 to its 1933–34 level. In addition, enrollment fell to its lowest point since the School opened, with 237 students.

During Campus Day in May 1933, work began on a sixty-by-ninety-foot pool in the small gulch above Ashland Street (behind the Administration Building), roughly where the library stands now. The project was the idea of Wayne Wells, who conceived of the pool as an adjunct to his biology courses.

In 1933, both Walter Redford and Arthur Taylor received their PhDs, Redford from the University of Washington and Taylor from the University of Southern California.

In February 1934, an evaluator visited the School from the American Association of Teachers Colleges. The evaluator was Dr. Henry Rockwell, president of Buffalo State Teachers College in New York. Rockwell's report noted that junior college students made up about a third of the total enrollment and that there was no extension work available for elementary teachers. He said faculty preparation was short of the standard, because 44 percent had less than a master's degree, only three faculty in the training school had bachelor's degrees, and the rest had none. He also said the library standard was violated, with only 5,692 volumes. However, he thought the practice teaching program was excellent and ended up recommending accreditation, which was duly granted.

During the spring 1934 term, the School added fifty new courses to the curriculum to strengthen the junior college offerings. This included an expansion of coursework in the sciences and two years of French and German. It was also during this term that Ollie Depew organized a literary society called Lambda Chi.

President Redford felt that enrollment had fallen because of economic conditions, but he thought the increasing number of high school graduates coming along would help compensate for the loss. He also felt the junior college program might boost enrollment by accepting students who did not qualify for teacher training. He was right on both counts; enrollment rose 21 percent in 1934–35.

Despite the increase in enrollment, the Institution was still struggling with reduced funding. At this point, the Ways and Means Committee of the state legislature contemplated shifting another half-million dollars out of the higher education budget. This led to a statewide discussion in which the closing of SONS was seriously considered. Fortunately, nothing came of it, and school went on.

Perhaps the most significant long-range development at this time grew out of Angus Bowmer's efforts to produce Shakespeare's plays on an Elizabethan stage. Starting early in the spring term, Bowmer had a stage built in four units in the auditorium. His student, Bob Stedman, played a central role in the construction. Stedman was shortly to be elected the student body president, and he later went on to a long and distinguished career as a high school teacher in Medford. The enterprise was broader than the Institution itself, as citizens from Medford, Phoenix, and Ashland participated along with the SONS students in both the building and the acting. On May 10 and 11, they produced *The Merchant of Venice*. Bowmer not only

Cast from Angus Bowmer's 1940 production of A Day with Shakespeare

directed, but he also played the part of Shylock—perhaps his favorite role. Two days later, the entire set was disassembled and moved to Klamath Falls for a performance on May 14. But it did not stop there: Bowmer had held discussions with a number of Ashland leaders and businessmen about reviving an old Ashland tradition that had fallen by the wayside—a community-wide Fourth of July celebration. Bowmer proposed that a stage be set up in the old Chautauqua shell. The city cooperated by contributing $400 and allowing a crew of ten men to build the stage according to Bowmer's instructions. *The Merchant of Venice* was shown again, and *Twelfth Night* was added. This was the beginning of what was to become the Oregon Shakespeare Festival (OSF).

There is a story that Bowmer loved to tell about this beginning. The committee in charge of the celebration was so sure the plays would lose money that they arranged for several boxing matches to cover any financial loss. As it turned out, it was the boxing that lost money, and the plays made enough money to cover the losses.

The developments in drama were not the only noteworthy events of the year. The highway in front of the campus was widened with a ten-foot strip of concrete on each side of the existing two-lane blacktop. After three years at SONS, Howard Hobson accepted the position of basketball coach at the University of Oregon. And the Public Works Administration of the U.S. government allotted $40,000 for a gymnasium at SONS.

A good year all around, 1935–36 saw enrollment increase by 5.5 percent. The chancellor set up a committee to plan for faculty ranking, including SONS faculty members Taylor and Wells. They decided that the associate professorship would be given to those with doctorates, since these individuals already had considerable experience. Those with master's degrees were made assistant professors, and those with bachelor's degrees or the equivalent were called instructors. There were several exceptions to these general rules. A. E. Strange, who possessed no degrees, was made an associate professor, as was Ida Belle O'Brien, who held a master's degree. On the other hand, two of the education faculty who had master's degrees remained at the instructor level. Experience was undoubtedly the determining factor in all of the exceptions. This faculty ranking system went into effect for 1935–36, and shortly thereafter tenure was also established.

Library holdings had been increased to more than 7,000 volumes, and interlibrary loans became available for the first time. The School established a Publicity Bureau, with Ollie Depew in charge. Two students with journalism experience, Maxine Gearhart and Virginia High, assisted her.

The new coach, Jean Eberhart, got off to a rousing start with national publicity. This was due to the SONS defeat of Albany College, 14–0. That happened to be Albany's twenty-eighth consecutive loss, which was a new national record, and sports editors all over the U.S. picked up the story.

To raise the standards for teachers, the state legislature passed a law requiring elementary education students graduating after January 1937 to have seven quarters of work; after January 1939, the requirement became eight quarters; and after January 1941, it would be nine quarters, or three years of study.

Construction began at long last on the gymnasium, and work was also undertaken to revamp Fuller Field. This included leveling it, creating a running track around the football field, and building a grandstand. The whole project was a testimonial to community cooperation. Student funds covered the material costs. The National Youth Administration supplied the labor. Ashland showed its support with a bulldozer and driver, as did the Forest Service with a large bulldozer. And the county engineer provided transportation for the equipment.

The year ended on a happy academic note. Miss Depew was notified that Ginn and Company would publish her textbook on children's literature.

In his report to the director of elementary teacher training, Redford pointed out for the first time that he was responsible to the director for curriculum administration, but that he was "directly responsible" to the chancellor for the budget and for physical plant and personnel administration.

In 1936–37, enrollment dropped by almost 20 percent, followed by another drop in 1937–38. The new gymnasium was completed and dedicated on October 19, 1936. Fuller Field was turfed in early 1937. The old normal school property was sold to Lottie Beswick for $2,500 in 1937, and the money was used to install removable bleachers in the gymnasium that could seat 1,750 children, or 1,500 adults. By now, the gymnasium was being called the Health and PE Building, and in December 1937, excavation began under the building to provide space for a chemistry laboratory and a boxing and wrestling room, as well as additional storage space. This work was done by WPA labor.

The library collection was expanded, with 8,666 volumes by June 1938. And the junior college program added more courses. Back in 1932, the junior college enrollment came to 2.5 percent of the total enrollment. By 1938, it made up 36 percent of the total. In May 1938, the Institution's first annual yearbook, the *Oregon Son*, went to press (in 1937, there had been a four-page "memory book"). In his biennial report, the president was able to say that the Shakespearean Festival had become an annual event sponsored by SONS. He also noted that the NYA-funded program was helping many of the students.

In 1938–39, enrollment rose 24 percent, with 247 students. Student costs went up, too—almost 60 percent—to twenty-two dollars per term for residents and twenty-eight dollars for nonresidents. The country was still in the depths of the Depression. Room and board cost six dollars per week, and books and supplies cost about ten dollars per term. Marshall Woodell took over as the registrar in 1939, filling the position left open by the death of Katherine Vincent, the original registrar of the Institution.

There were some encouraging developments, also. Faculty salaries rose to the level they had reached in 1932, but they remained at these levels until 1943. In 1938, Southern Oregon Normal School finally received full accreditation from the American Association of Teachers Colleges. In 1939, Governor Sprague signed into law the bill changing the Institution's name to Southern Oregon College of Education (SOCE).

The 1939–40 academic year showed another increase in enrollment, up just 9 percent. However, catastrophe hit the athletic program: the football program was dropped. Due in part to poor

Civil Aeronautics class from the 1939-40 Oregon Son *yearbook*

attendance at the games, the program was experiencing financial difficulties and could no longer be sustained.

At the other extreme, the College began offering a course in Civil Aeronautics. Congress had authorized a program for training civilian pilots at selected educational institutions, including SOCE. Ground school required seventy-two hours of fieldwork, and advanced training with flight instruction took place at the Medford Airport. The program lasted three years.

SOCE students enjoyed an opportunity to participate in the Oregon Shakespeare Festival this year. There were other opportunities, it seems, open to some students. A considerable stir was caused when Martha Hassett, an eighteen-year-old SOCE freshman, was chosen as the model for an advertisement that appeared in the *Saturday Evening Post*, one of the leading national magazines of the time. The ad was created by the Travel Department of the Oregon State Highway Commission.

The year ended with three firsts: commencement was held in the College gymnasium; both students and faculty wore academic regalia; and, lastly, Professor A.E. Strange retired and was the first to be given a half-salary pension, which in his case came to $1,700 per year.

In the 1940–41 year, enrollment was down 16 percent to 225 students, beginning a downward slide that continued throughout the war years. Student costs dropped as well, with tuition and fees going from $22 to $18.50 for residents and from $28 to $24.50 for nonresidents. Two new faculty members arrived: Otto Wilda in art and Stephen Epler in education and as dean of men. Epler was already widely known as the inventor of six-man football, which he developed while an instructor at a Nebraska high school. It was not long, therefore, before a four-team league of intramural six-man football was organized at SOCE.

It was in this academic year that SOCE was authorized to offer the bachelor of science degree in elementary education, beginning in January 1941. This is one of the Institution's great landmarks, along with gaining the title of "college." At last, a four-year degree program became available. The president noted that there was now an approved campus plan, which included a women's dormitory and a library building, both of which he anticipated "to come" soon. In this case, "soon" turned out to be a decade away.

What intervened, of course, was World War II. It can be easily understood that the war created havoc in most institutions of higher education, and SOCE was especially vulnerable. The overarching reality of the war years was the constant attrition of students. Enrollment fell 16 percent in 1941, 35 percent in 1942, and 60 percent in 1943, reaching a low of forty-five students in the spring 1944 term, with just a few males among them. This encouraged the election of the first woman, Henrietta Hall from Gerber, California, to the student body presidency in 1943. Since the School's inception, women had always held an overwhelming majority at the Institution, yet the students had always elected males to the highest office.

As the student body shrank during these years, so too did the faculty and the budget. Of the sixteen faculty members not associated with the Lincoln School, eight were in the armed services or working for the Red Cross (Taylor). That cleared out all of the men, except McNeal and Wells, who were both too old to serve. Given the budget cuts, President Redford commented that it was "fortunate" that so many staff members were on leave without pay in the service. The cuts hurt so much that in the summer of 1942, six of the faculty women took unpaid leaves of absence to help the Institution cope with a budget reduction, which was followed by another 10-percent budget reduction in 1943–44.

There were other losses as well. The athletic program disappeared. There were no yearbooks issued between 1942 and 1946. There was no catalog for the 1943–44 academic year. The last printed *Siskiyou* came out in April 1943 and was not back in print until February 1946. In December 1943, and again in December 1944, the *Siskiyou* appeared as a six-page mimeographed newsletter.

But all was not lost. In 1941, the Board of Higher Education met in Ashland and authorized a two-year secretarial science program leading to an associate of science (AS) degree at SOCE. In December 1942, the College was "provisionally accredited" as a degree-granting institution by the Northwest Association of Schools and Colleges, and it was fully accredited in December 1943. In March 1944, the American Association of Teachers Colleges granted accreditation. And in 1945, two-year AS degree programs were added for medical and dental assistants and for merchandising. In addition, three new courses in "home arts" covered clothing construction, food preparation, and personal and family relationships. Further, the library collection had not been neglected, for the 1945 catalog listed 19,464 volumes, an increase of more than 10,000 volumes since 1940, or more than double the earlier collection.

The president's report for 1940–42 stated that the "same general philosophy as always prevailed," but there was now an added emphasis on "the significance and importance of the ideals and principles of the American way of life," especially "when the enemies of democracy are trying to destroy them." Redford pointed out that the unfinished portions of the PE building basement had been developed, with the help of the Works Progress Administration (WPA), into additional PE facilities that contributed to the physical fitness phase of the general defense program. Mathematics, physics, and chemistry courses were added to the curriculum to help students prepare for defense or military jobs. Redford also noted that the College was participating in the Navy V-1 and the Army Air Corps Enlisted Reserve programs and that seventy-eight students had completed Civil Pilot Training, with most of them now serving in the Army or naval air forces. Redford reported that most students had completed first-aid training, along with many community members.

In his 1943–44 report, Redford wrote that all of the men in the reserve programs had been called up, leaving only a few seventeen-year-olds on campus. He also noted that the Civil Pilot Training program had been closed. Redford observed that the war had interrupted plans for a women's dormitory and library building, and he hoped that those plans would be carried out after the war was won and the budget restored.

There was an improvement in enrollment in the 1945–46 year. Seventy-two students registered, which was a 22-percent increase, although the numbers were still small. The local paper reported the death of J.A. Churchill, the College's first president, on February 3, 1945. In October 1945, the *Ashland Daily Tidings* lamented the lagging enrollment at SOCE, pointing out that almost four times as many students were enrolled at EOCE. They complained that nothing was being done to revitalize SOCE and that such efforts were badly needed, faulting the state board for not taking action. This was followed a week later by a notice that Redford would retire from the presidency of SOCE on January 1, 1946, and that he would be succeeded by Dr. Elmo Stevenson from Oregon State College.

Elmo Stevenson

Elmo Stevenson was born in Yuba, California, on February 25, 1904. He was the first westerner and the first one born in the twentieth century to assume the presidency at SOCE. He earned his BA at San Jose State College in 1927. Stevenson went on to attend Stanford University, where he earned an MA in 1929 and an EdD in 1939. He worked for the Oregon State System of Higher Education (OSSHE) as an assistant professor of science at EOCE from 1929 to 1940, before moving to Oregon State College as the professor of science education, a post he held until his appointment as president of SOCE.

Upon Stevenson's appointment, the board indicated that he would have to boost enrollment at the College or they would be forced to close it. This provided a powerful incentive. There had been 72 students in the fall term. Enrollment rose to 154 by winter and 203 by spring. The new president was having some effect, and he was working at it. In the first two months of his presidency, Stevenson gave speeches at twenty-one meetings in nine cities: Ashland, Coos Bay, Eugene, Grants Pass, Klamath Falls, Medford, Portland, Salem, and Yreka. He continued this way for years, and it paid off. Wherever three people were gathered, there was Elmo selling the College.

Things were beginning to pick up on campus, too. The *Siskiyou* resumed publication in February 1946. Stevenson announced that basketball, baseball, football, and track programs would resume the following year. Male faculty were returning from their service assignments, and students were coming in from the service as well. About 77 percent of the male students were veterans, and enrollment in the junior college program and the secretarial science program accounted for 64 percent of the total enrollment. Stevenson complained bitterly and publicly that salaries were too low. He was paid $5,270 per year. Associate professors earned $3,370, and assistant professors earned $2,970 for twelve-month contracts. There were no full professors.

In a July 1946 report to the state board, Stevenson detailed the "College War Record in World War II." Seven faculty men had served in the military, and one in the Red Cross. Nearly 500 alumni men had served in the armed forces, with eight reported fatalities. He wrote that there were inadequate records for other former students, making it impossible to tell how many had actually served. Both staff and students had helped out with the local USO programs and presented programs at Camp White. The staff had also assisted with the state's teacher shortage by encouraging two-year students to take emergency certification.

In the first of his regular reports to the state board, Stevenson declared that the College had three functions: degree work in elementary education, junior college work, and four 2-year terminal programs. He felt strongly that there should also be one 2-year terminal program in agriculture, especially horticulture, but this was denied. Enrollment was rising, but now men—mostly veterans—outnumbered women by more than two to one, and only a third of the students were in education. Of the seven faculty members who had served in the military, five returned and two resigned. Former coach Jean Eberhart went into business in Ashland, opening a sporting goods store. Stephen Epler accepted the position of director of the Vanport Extension Center in Portland, which ultimately became Portland State College under his guidance. The number of staff was back to its prewar level, and they were given raises ranging from $150 to $300 for the coming biennium. But rising enrollments also led to a need for more faculty. Indeed, Stevenson anticipated more than 400 students for the fall 1946 term. As a result, he projected increased needs for both facilities and curricular expansion. A women's dormitory was essential, and plans for it were underway. The College required additional classroom and library space, as well as improved science facilities. Stevenson wanted new courses in engineering, advanced biology and chemistry, Spanish, and journalism. He proposed a guidance program with a testing bureau and counseling center for veterans. The Veterans Public Housing Administration had agreed, he reported, to provide twenty-eight family units for married veterans and a dormitory for sixty-four single veterans. Finally, in his report, Stevenson reminded the board that the faculty was currently on twelve-month contracts and should be changed to ten-month contracts, with higher salaries and additional pay for summers.

THE STEVENSON YEARS

WE COME NOW to 1946–47, Stevenson's first full year as president of the College. That was the year I joined the faculty, and I have been involved in College affairs ever since. I shall try to be as objective as possible about everything that occurred. I cannot help but speak of myself when I was personally involved, however, and I beg the reader's understanding and forgiveness in these cases. First, therefore, a few words about how I came to be here.

When I was discharged from the U.S. Army in November 1945, I went home to Boston. Since the school year was already well underway, it was a difficult time for a teacher to enter the job market. I wrote a teacher's agency in Denver, and shortly after I received notice that an English teacher was needed in Lakeview, Oregon, starting on January 1, 1946. I applied and was hired. I became good friends with the superintendent of schools at Lakeview, Cleon Caldwell, who had graduated from Southern Oregon Normal School in 1929.

So I was familiar with the College when a prominent member of the Lakeview community, Margaret Kucera, contacted Stevenson about me. Having been a student with Stevenson at Oregon State, this woman told him there was a young man teaching in Lakeview whom he should consider for the College. Stevenson came out to visit me in March, and he promptly hired me. I finished the year in Lakeview in May, then returned to Boston to start a doctoral program, reappearing in Ashland with my wife and two sons in September.

In the fall term of 1946, much of what President Stevenson had hoped and worked for came to pass. Enrollment exceeded his expectations, coming in at 519 students; the faculty more than doubled; and a new program in radio-electric service and management was added to the curriculum. The library collection stood at 19,893 volumes, and student expenses per term came to twenty-four dollars for tuition and fees for in-state students, and thirty-four dollars for out-of-state students. Room and board was ten dollars per week, and total book costs averaged about ten dollars. Construction of veteran's housing began on seven 4-family units for married veterans and one 64-man dormitory for single veterans. The buildings had been trucked down from East Vanport, near Portland, and were completed for use by November. They were erected just east of the Administration Building, roughly in the area where the Schneider Museum of Art (SMA) now stands, forming what became known as "Vets Village."

Of the fifteen new faculty members, seven spent the rest of their working careers at the College. This includes Mabel Winston, who became registrar and dean of women in early 1946. Five men also started in fall 1946: Elliott MacCracken, instructor in mathematics; Glenn Matthews, instructor in music; Leon Mulling, instructor in English; Lloyd Pennington, instructor in science; and me, instructor in English and languages. Eugene Bowman, instructor in mathematics, arrived in winter 1947.

Harold Bishop, who came as athletic director and stayed for two years, was among the eight faculty members who did not stay on permanently. He originated the term "Pear Bowl" for a post-season football game, and he suggested that the field behind the College, which was planted in radishes, be used to build a stadium. An alumnus who had earned a degree from Stanford University, Edmund Dews taught in the sciences. In December 1946, Dews was named a Rhodes Scholar. Russell Elliott, instructor in history, arrived with his doctorate and was with the College for five years, leaving to join the faculty at the University of Nevada. Marie Ferraris taught Spanish and French; she married shortly after her arrival and became Marie Boyden. She spent five years at the College. Robert Monroe, another graduate of SOCE, became a librarian. He was with the College for two years and left for advanced study at the University of Washington, where he remained as a librarian. The football coach, Alexander Simpson, who had been a coach at Ashland and Medford High Schools, left the College in 1951. Clifford Williams came to take charge of Lincoln School and the education program. After three years, he accepted a job in Portland. Finally, John Morlan took over as the business manager of the College for two years.

This group of new people outnumbered the old faculty. Suddenly, the College seemed like a new and different place. But the "old-timers" were most welcoming, hospitable, and helpful. Indeed, the newcomers regarded McNeal, Taylor, and Wells with considerable admiration and respect. Two others, Otto Wilda and Marshall Woodell—who had been at the College before the war but had gone into the services—fit right in with the newcomers.

President Stevenson was a man of firm ideas about faculty responsibilities and standards. Of course, it was expected that faculty would do their best with teaching assignments and advising stu-

Elmo Stevenson

dents. But that was only the beginning. Faculty were assigned extracurricular responsibilites in addition to full course loads. Thus, Mulling became the *Siskiyou* advisor. Elliott was put in charge of moving furniture into the new dormitory, and so on. I was given the task of writing sports publicity, as well as assisting in the Testing Bureau. Faculty members were expected to be on duty from 8 a.m. to 5 p.m. They were to be dressed properly: shirts, ties, and coats or jackets for men, dresses or skirts and blouses for women. Men were to be clean-shaven, and they were strongly urged to join service clubs—Rotary, Lions, and Kiwanis were the most popular—and tender some sort of service to the community. All were urged to make public speeches at every opportunity. Those lacking doctorates were strongly urged to obtain one as soon as possible.

Faculty members of the twenty-first century will, no doubt, find some of these policies quite astonishing. However, most of us at that time were glad to do what the president wanted. There was some griping about the twelve-month contract—standard for most of the faculty—because it resulted in lower salaries than faculty at other OSSHE institutions, who earned the same or higher for only a nine- or ten-month contract. There were also complaints about the unusually heavy teaching loads. At this time, a 15- or 16-credit teaching load was standard, and some faculty even carried 18-credit loads in addition to all of the other duties and expectations mentioned above.

The president's wishes bore fruit rapidly. Many of the faculty became active in the community, and of the seven new faculty members who stayed on at the College, six achieved their doctoral degrees within a few years, as did four of the old-timers.

At this point, a general description of conditions in Ashland and at the College is in order. In 1946, Ashland was a community of about 6,000 people. It was a strong railroad town, serving as the central point along the main line between Sacramento and Portland. There was a roundhouse, a freight house, and a depot. The railroad people made up an important contingent of the local population. But passenger service ended in 1938 when the main line of railroad traffic shifted to Klamath Falls to avoid the arduous pull over the Siskiyou Mountains. There was still one train a day to Portland and back, but even this was discontinued in 1952. The result, of course, was a severe drop in railroad employment in Ashland. Subsequently, a number of sawmills operating in and around town and the logging operations that supplied them became the major employers. The Bagley Canning Company, which canned a great variety of locally grown fruits and vegetables, and the Newbry Orchards, which maintained a sizeable fruit packing plant, also provided local employment. And there was the Oak Street Tank and Steel Company, which produced tanks of different sizes for various purposes. These are all gone now.

Not only were the teaching loads heavy at the College, but there were also no limits on class size. It was not unusual to have forty-five students in an English Composition class. Later, such courses were limited to twenty-five. Some instructors had to carry five such classes—later limited to three. Since it was standard to assign a theme a week, these instructors spent most of their weekends grading papers.

At this time, instructors were supposed to grade on a normal curve. While many instructors tried to approximate this, almost no one had as many F's as A's. In general, grades were based on a 100-point scale: 90 or better was an A, 80–89 was a B, 60–79 a C, 50–59 a D, and under 50 an F. This represents a high standard for achievement and understanding, and few indeed were the students who could boast of a straight-A record.

While hired for their expertise in a particular field, faculty members sometimes ended up with teaching assignments outside their original specialization. Thus, Arthur Taylor taught classes in history, political science, sociology, and mathematics—all during the same term. Wayne Wells taught biology, physics, and mathematics. Another taught literature, history, and economics. Yet another taught writing, speech, and drama. I covered literature, philosophy, and German. And thus it went. Faculty of this time were often "all over the lot."

Part of the reason for this was the lack of "departments." The catalog listed "English," but that included courses in speech, journalism, theatre arts, writing, and literature. "Science" included all of the sciences, while "mathematics" was listed separately. "Social Science" covered economics, geography, history, political science, and sociology. Only two foreign languages were offered: French and German.

During this period, everyone was directly responsible to the president. If faculty members wanted or needed anything, they went to the president. Stevenson knew what everyone was doing. Some felt this was too autocratic. And yet, in my experience, no faculty member with an idea or a project was ever turned down, but was instead given whatever help possible. This continued for many years, even after some departments were created.

In 1946, all of the newly hired faculty members were given the ranking of instructor. The three oldest of the faculty—McNeal, Taylor, and Wells—were associate professors, while the remaining old-timers were assistant professors. There were no professors. The faculty salaries at this time were still on a twelve-month basis. The top salary for men (associate professors with doctorates) was $3,750, while the top salary for women was $3,300. Newly hired instructors received $3,000. The president earned $6,250.

On the academic side, the general education requirements for the BS degree in elementary education (the only degree offered) consisted of:

English Composition (9 credits)
Foundations of Physical Science (9 credits)
Biological Science Survey (9 credits)
Background of Social Science (9 credits)
Orientation (1 credit)
Personal Hygiene (2 credits)
Essentials of Speech (3 credits)
Foundations of Mathematics (3 credits)
Physical Education (6 credits; 1 each term for two years)
World Literature (9 credits)
Social Science (9 credits chosen from history, economics,
    or sociology)
General Psychology (9 credits)
Geography (9 credits)

Since students also had to complete Introduction to Education (3 credits) in the second year, the general education requirement totaled 90 credits of required work, leaving only 6 credits for electives during that second year.

Lloyd Pennington (back to camera) teaching his Organic Chemistry class at the House of Mystery, March 1948

The work in psychology and geography was viewed as part of the preparation for education rather than part of general education. Orientation emphasized adjustment to college, use of the library, proper study habits, and related topics. This course seemed to make a good deal of sense for beginning college students, and its ultimate disappearance from the catalog by 1950 was a serious loss. This also applies to several other courses: Foundations of Physical Science presented a yearlong introduction to astronomy, chemistry, geology, and physics. It continued to be offered until 1968. Background of Social Science, another yearlong course, introduced students to the study of economics, history, political science, and sociology. This course was dropped in 1963 upon the arrival of a new chair of social science. World Literature, originally required for all students, ceased being a general requirement in 1960. I cannot help regarding all of these cancelled courses as unfortunate losses for the students. They gave beginning students insights into what was available in academia and an opportunity to discover which subjects appealed to them.

In World Literature, students were introduced to the Bible and the classical Greek and Roman writers, as well as the major authors of European literatures, such as Cervantes, Dante, Goethe, Rousseau, and Tolstoy. The course prepared students who wanted to continue in English or American literature to read and understand many modern authors.

Why did we lose all that? As faculty increasingly became specialists in one discipline, they concentrated on that discipline alone. Physicists wanted to teach physics, economists wanted to teach economics, English literature specialists wanted to teach English literature. No one was interested in what were regarded as shallow, grab-bag courses.

Other practices ultimately vanished, too. From 1946 to 1962, there was an assembly held every week in the auditorium on the top floor of Churchill Hall. It was "expected" that all students and faculty would attend. A fifty-minute program featured local or visiting speakers or performers lecturing on a wide variety of topics. The president usually made some remarks and introduced the program. In 1962, "expected" was changed to "encouraged," and after 1967, assemblies were dropped entirely. This was essentially a matter of

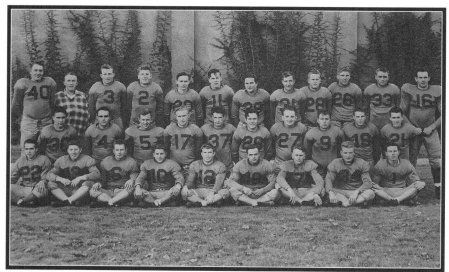

1946-47 Red Raiders

numbers. The 1946 enrollment of just more than 500 became almost 1,500 by 1962, and it exceeded 3,000 by 1967. Mulkey Hall, the Churchill auditorium, could not come close to holding the entire student body, nor could the gymnasium, where assemblies were transferred in the later years of the program.

The saddest event of the 1946–47 academic year occurred in March. An excavation had been dug for the foundation of the new women's dormitory (to be Susanne Homes Hall). It was more than 100 feet long, 50 feet wide, and 6 feet deep. During the unusually heavy rainy season, it filled with water, and there seven-year-old Donald Philips, who lived on nearby Indiana Street, drowned. Apparently, he had been trying to float on a mattress and had fallen off or tipped over. People on campus felt heartsick about the incident.

At the other extreme was the unprecedented success of the College football team. This is well worth describing in some detail.

Fifty-five men, many of them war veterans, had turned out for football to play for Coach Alexander Simpson. There being no other facilities, practice was conducted on the hill in front of what is now Central Hall, and the joke of the time was that players needed to have one leg shorter than the other. Games were played on Ashland, Medford, and Grants Pass high school fields. This was the first football team after an eight-year lapse, and it was clad in the School colors of red and gold. The newspaper sportswriters of the time began calling them by the old name "SONS" (for Southern Oregon Normal School). Being in charge of sports publicity, I felt strongly that this name would not do, so I sent out stories calling the team the "Red Raiders of the Rogue." The sports editors objected to the length of that title and quickly cut it down to "Red Raiders." By the end of October, everyone was using that title, and I felt gratified that I had contributed it. The team won eight games, defeating such opponents as Chico State, Humboldt State, San Francisco State, and Central Washington. The last game, against Central Washington, was a special invitational game called the Pear Bowl, which set a precedent for more such games in the future. This was the first— and so far the only—undefeated, untied football team in the College's history.

With the great growth of student enrollment and the doubling of the faculty, space was at a premium. There were many unsatisfactory conditions. For example, a chemistry laboratory operated in the gymnasium basement. A faculty office was set up on the top floor of the Administration Building; it contained eight desks for eight faculty members, all in one medium-sized room that had once been a small classroom. Earlier, I mentioned the former military buildings from Vanport, brought in to house married students (Vets Village) and provide a dormitory for male veterans. Two other buildings had been set up at the same time. The first was called Science Hall, later named Pine Hall. It contained chemistry and physics laboratories, a darkroom, faculty offices, and a large lecture room. It also housed the College Testing Bureau and the Veterans Administration Guidance Center. Next to it was the Student Union, later named Myrtle Hall, which contained a lounge and snack bar, as well as a co-op food store and a home economics laboratory. Both of these buildings stood behind the Administration Building.

To help students improve their reading abilities, a two-week test project was set up involving seventy students. At the beginning of the project, students were reading an average of 269 words a minute with an 86-percent comprehension level. By the end of the two weeks, they were reading an average of 357 words a minute with a 94-percent comprehension level. These results were good enough to suggest that a reading clinic would be helpful to students, and the following year such a clinic was established.

Susanne Homes Hall

In addition, Leon Mulling began to help students needing special speech instruction. That same year, Science Hall, the Student Union, and Susanne Homes Hall (the women's dormitory) went into operation. Spanish and general engineering were added to the curriculum. Student costs were up slightly. Tuition and fees per term came to twenty-four dollars for residents and thirty-four dollars for nonresidents, room and board was twelve dollars per week, and books cost about fifteen dollars per term. The students that year came from

Churchill Hall

twenty-three states, with students from Alaska and Hawaii counting as residents.

In early 1947, I approached President Stevenson with the suggestion that the Administration Building be named to commemorate former President Churchill, who had passed away in 1945. Stevenson thought this was a good idea and proposed it to the State Board of Higher Education, which approved it in fall 1947, making "Churchill Hall" the official name. Other events of some lasting import include the closing of Ashland Street, which originally ran directly through the campus just behind Churchill Hall, and the changing of faculty contracts from twelve months to ten months per year.

Faculty contracts had been the source of an often acrimonious battle between the faculty and the president for more than a year. At one point, during a heated confrontation between a faculty committee and the president in Churchill Hall's public corridor—with students passing back and forth—one of the senior faculty members called the president an S.O.B. in a loud voice. To his credit, Stevenson never held this against the faculty member. Other administrators might have fired him on the spot. But this man received his raises and promotions as they were due. This kindled the respect and admiration I had developed for Stevenson. While researching this history, I read through Stevenson's papers and reports to the state board. I discovered, with some shock, that he had been requesting that the board change faculty contracts to ten months well before the faculty even made it an issue. This was typical of him. Stevenson's sense of loyalty to the board caused him to take all of the heat and venom from the faculty, without passing it on to the board.

Also in 1947, the first professorships were created. The distribution of ranks for the faculty stood at 32 percent instructors, 40 percent assistant professors, 18 percent associate professors, and 10 percent professors.

This faculty was active in the community. The president reported proudly to the board that faculty had delivered 393 talks to organizations and given 72 radio addresses, noting that the College was represented in every service organization in the area.

By the following year (1948–49), the library holdings had grown slightly to 20,848 volumes, and Stevenson was lobbying heavily for a new library. He had also been complaining to the board that faculty salaries were too low, which led to a 15-percent raise for faculty. Prices rose for the students, with tuition and fees per term going to twenty-nine dollars for residents and thirty-nine dollars for nonresidents. Room and board was listed at fourteen dollars per week, and the cost of books per term rose to twenty-five dollars.

It was in this year that the Shakespeare Festival started by Angus Bowmer attracted the attention of Stanford University's Margery

Bailey, whom Bowmer had first met at Stanford before the war. She arranged for Stanford's Dramatists Alliance to send the College a gift of books, which became the core of what is now called the Margery Bailey Renaissance Collection. From 1949 until her death in 1963,

Bailey came to Ashland in the summers to participate in the Oregon Shakespeare Festival and serve as its academic guide on Shakespeare's period in history. A specialist in renaissance studies, Bailey founded the Institute of Renaissance Studies in 1950. Every summer, the Institute offered courses centering on the plays being produced by the festival, and outstanding scholars presented lectures on Shakespeare and his times. Students could enroll in these courses at either SOCE or Stanford. This program was the ancestor of what is now the University's Center for Shakespeare Studies.

Angus Bowmer

In 1949–50, the faculty received another salary increase, this time 12 percent. A boxing program was initiated, and the student body voted to use a Viking warrior as the symbol for the College's Red Raiders. Ten of Oregon's American Association of University Professors (AAUP) chapters, in both public and private institutions, voted to organize a statewide association, of which I was elected president.

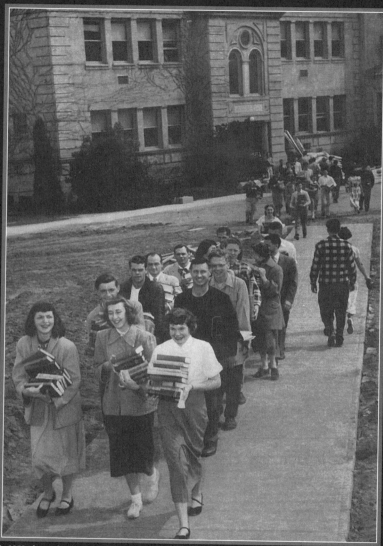

*In 1950, the student body and faculty turned out to move the library collection
from Churchill Hall to the new library building.*

THE 1950s

In 1950, the state board purchased a home for the president of the College on Elkader Street. The home, which overlooked the campus, had belonged to a physician who retired and left Ashland. After the house was refurbished, Stevenson and his family moved in from their home on Avery Street.

It was in this year that the new library-classroom building (now Central Hall) was completed and opened for service. The student body and faculty turned out to move the library from Churchill Hall to the new building. It was an amazing display of cooperative effort. People carried armloads of books from one building to the other, and within eight hours, some 32,000 books and 300 periodicals had been moved and ensconced in their proper places. The library was ready for business the following day.

The first appointment of an academic administrator was made when John McAulay was appointed director of teacher education. The College also reached a high point in enrollment with 812 registered students.

In 1951–52, everyone was dismayed when only 583 students enrolled. It was a great blow. Before the board, Stevenson explained that enrollment was down because most of the World War II veterans had graduated, the Korean War was taking a toll on students, and there was a dip in high school graduates. But he predicted the enrollment would come up again. It finally did, but not until 1955, when 816 students enrolled.

During the 1951–52 academic year, the College opened an annex to Susanne Homes Hall, started a broadcasting program with a small radio station in the library basement, inaugurated tennis as a new campus sport, and approved the Master's in Elementary Education

Program. Some graduate work at last. Best of all for faculty, salaries were boosted by a heartening 22 percent.

In 1952–53, the library was made an official depository for U.S. government documents. Enrollment was down again (548). Alva Graham was appointed director of graduate studies, and chairs were appointed for English (me), Physical Education and Health (Daniel Bulkley), Science-Mathematics (Wayne Wells), and Social Science (Arthur Taylor). These units were called departments at the time.

One of the important events of 1953–54 was the state board's elimination of the director of elementary education position. The president of the Oregon College of Education (OCE) at Monmouth had held this position. Under the old system, the president of Southern Oregon College of Education was responsible to the president of OCE. This had become increasingly awkward, and it was now pointless as well, since SOCE had just been given the right to award degrees in secondary education and general studies. This merits some explanation.

For some years, most of the younger faculty members had wanted the College to develop programs in the liberal arts and sciences and to ultimately establish majors in their own disciplines. Politics prevented the achievement of this goal. SOCE was a small sub-unit in a much larger state system, and many of the old guard at the University of Oregon and Oregon State College opposed allowing the liberal arts and sciences to spread throughout the system. So SOCE developed a new academic vocabulary to get around this roadblock. The liberal arts and sciences became "General Studies." Additionally, since separate subject majors were forbidden, subjects were grouped under three broad headings: "Humanities," "Science-Mathematics," and "Social Science." This enabled the College to start the liberal arts and science programs.

It was in this year that the School colors changed to red and black. The College was also given the opportunity to do some pioneering work in educational television through the courtesy of William Smullin, the general manager of station KBES (now KOBI) in Medford. Smullin gave SOCE a half-hour of prime time every week throughout the academic year. That first year, Donald MacDougall of the Social Science Department presented a course in American history. Over the following three years, I presented courses in world literature, philosophy, and comparative religion.

In 1954–55, SOCE included graduate-level work other than education in the curriculum for the first time. The student body voted to change the College symbol from a Viking to an Indian. (For more than thirty years, the Indian represented the College at its sporting events, finally retiring in the early 1980s. By that time, the Indian was viewed as politically incorrect and offensive to the local Native Americans. The College went without a mascot until 1997, when President Stephen Reno decided to give the University a new mascot: the red-tailed hawk.)

In 1956, the name of the Institution was changed to Southern Oregon College (SOC), indicating that the Institution was no longer just a school of education, although that continued to be a vital function. At this same time, what had previously been called "departments" became three liberal arts academic divisions, with subject-specific departments established within them. Wells, Taylor, and I served as chairs of the Science-Mathematics Division, the Social Science Division, and the Humanities Division, respectively. Separate disciplines were indicated within each division: botany, chemistry, physics, and zoology in Science-Mathematics; economics, geography, history, psychology, and sociology in Social Science; and English, journalism, philosophy and religion, speech, theatre arts,

From the 1958 Raider *yearbook*

and writing in Humanities. For the first time, upper division work was made available in French, German, and Spanish. Also, a 'G' notation was added to some 400-level courses, meaning qualified students could take them for graduate credit.

Also for the first time, the faculty was granted the right to elect a Faculty Council to advise the administration. Seven representatives were chosen from the Institution's four divisions (Education, Humanities, Science-Mathematics, and Social Science), with no more than two from any division, to serve three-year terms.

In 1956–57, chairs were appointed for the Art, Music, and Business Education Departments. These were Marion Ady, Oscar Bjorlie, and Alvin Miller, respectively. Also in 1957, SOC opened the newly completed gymnasium as the Physical Education and Health Building (now McNeal Pavilion).

The next year, 1957–58, was a large growth year for the College's buildings. SOC opened the Science Building, Siskiyou Hall (a new men's dormitory), and the Siskiyou Commons. A heating plant went into operation, and the old gymnasium (Memorial Court) was remodeled and named the Britt Student Center. Additionally, Vets Village was moved across Siskiyou Boulevard to the north portion of campus and renamed College Court.

During the 1958–59 year, the College added courses in library science. It was also authorized to offer master's degree programs in secondary education. A foundation was established for fundraising. I was appointed to the new position of director of general studies. Since the designated teaching areas of humanities, science-mathematics, and social science all fell under "general studies," I called myself a poor man's dean of arts and sciences.

By the end of the decade, SOC had witnessed the following increases: Student enrollment had risen from 812 in 1950 to 1,259 in 1959; the thirty-seven faculty members at the beginning of the decade had become more than seventy; the 20,000-volume library now exceeded 40,000 volumes; and the twenty-four-acre campus had grown to seventy-five acres. Clearly, SOC had much to be proud of.

THE 1960s

At the beginning of the decade, President Stevenson reported to the state board that 50 percent of SOC's faculty held doctorates. He noted that the College employed fifty essential civil service employees, but the Institution needed more. SOC was also lacking books for the library, classrooms, land, and money for faculty salaries, which were still low compared to upstate institutions. Stevenson declared with pride that SOC student scores rated above the norms on the national examinations. Also at this time, Alvin Fellers was appointed director of student affairs, the first such official in the history of the College.

During the 1960–61 academic year, the first unit of the Cascade Complex was completed. By 1966, this new dormitory was expanded to nine units. The College created an Honors Program for students of superior scholastic ability. Supervised by a faculty Honors Council, this program included lower division honors courses and degree honors programs in all of the divisions.

In 1961–62, physical education courses became coed, moving the College toward gender equality. This was also the first year of the bachelor's degree in business. These programs would become increasingly important for SOC.

In his 1962 report to the state board, Stevenson continued to harp on the major needs of the College: additional facilities for health and physical education, classroom space, land, and research funds. He also called for a greater reduction of the salary differentials between SOC faculty and those at other institutions and a reduction of SOC's high student–teacher ratio. Given how these needs affected faculty in particular, it was remarkable that Stevenson could say in his report that "faculty spirit was excellent."

Responding to the financial trouble of the privately owned ski lodge, the College founded the Mt. Ashland Corporation in 1962. A wonderful community resource, the lodge fostered excellent winter sport, which many SOC faculty and students enjoyed. But the private enterprise was in serious financial trouble and at risk of going out of business, so Stevenson recruited a number of the area's leading businessmen to form the Mt. Ashland Corporation. They incorporated, formed a board of directors, and sold stock in the corporation, raising more than $200,000. The lodge and ski area remained in business, with the help of some SOC faculty and students, until 1967. By then, the corporation was making sufficient profit that private enterprise could again take control of it. The College had clearly saved the ski resort for the community.

In 1962, Speech and Theatre Arts was organized into a department, with Leon Mulling as its head. The term "head" now applied to those who administered departments.

The following year, the College opened a Student Health Center, with full-time medical and nursing professionals available.

John Trudeau, an assistant professor of music at Portland State College, visited Ashland and Jacksonville in the summer of 1963 and conceived the idea of presenting classical music concerts on a hillside in Jacksonville's Britt Gardens. The Music Department hastened to assist, and the College employed Trudeau for the following eight summers to develop Britt Festivals.

In the 1963–64 academic year, the state board granted the College permission to offer master's degrees in general studies and business education. The general studies degrees covered the three broad areas of humanities, science-mathematics, and social science. SOC was still not permitted to refer to specific subject-matter disciplines. Along with the master's degrees came such open-ended courses as Research, Thesis, Reading and Conference, and Seminar. These course titles provided faculty with the leeway to embark on a variety of scholarly endeavors. Two more department heads were named: Dennis Hannan for Modern Languages and Sheldon Rio for Mathematics. The faculty teaching load was at last reduced from 15 to 12 credits per term. In his 1964 report to the board, Stevenson bemoaned the fact that the College had "the lowest cost per student for everything" in the state system. He was far from proud of that, as some thought, and said, "This must be remedied if faculty morale and high quality instruction are to be attained." He requested support for a new library, another science building, higher salaries, more land, additional funds for research, and, finally, a reduction in the student–teacher ratio, which he said stood at 33:1.

In 1964–65, there were numerous developments destined to have an ongoing impact. A social science building was opened and quickly named Taylor Hall after long-time Professor of Social Science Arthur Samuel Taylor, who had passed away the previous year. At long last, the state board granted the College subject majors. The first were BA/BS degrees in biology, chemistry, English, and history, along with a BFA in theatre arts. Two more heads were named: Marvin Coffee for the Biology Department and Lloyd Pennington for the Chemistry Department. The Business Department gained division status, Richard Byrns succeeded me as head of the English Department, and I was named the director of liberal arts and sciences.

In 1965–66, the label "dean" began to be widely used, replacing "director." Thus, we had Alvin Fellers as dean of students, Esby McGill as dean of faculty, Bill Sampson as dean of education, and me as dean of arts and sciences. The Health and Physical Education Building gained an Olympic-sized swimming pool. The College added Russian language and anthropology to the curriculum. Also that year, Frederick Rosentreter was appointed head of the History Department. Three controversies, in particular, made 1965–66 especially interesting.

The first is the Adamian Case, and it became a considerable *cause célèbre*. In 1965, a young man named Paul Adamian was hired as an assistant professor of English. Also in 1965, the Oregon legislature passed a bill requiring all faculty members employed by the state to sign a loyalty oath (this was at the height of the McCarthy era). Those failing to sign were to have their salaries cut off. The president and the dean of faculty conducted themselves as they had been instructed by the state board, asking faculty to sign the loyalty oath. All of the faculty signed except Adamian. He objected to the oath on principle, and he went about raising an outcry at being penalized for not signing. He complained to the American Association of University Professors (AAUP) and the American Civil Liberties Union (ACLU). Both were happy to jump into the fray, and they sent investigating committees to the campus. Although they were only acting on instructions from the state board, President Stevenson and Dean McGill were portrayed as villains in the case.

Accordingly, Stevenson sent Adamian a letter of dismissal. It was at this point that I entered the case, as dean of arts and sciences. I had been absent from the campus during the summer and fall of 1965, enjoying a sabbatical in Europe. I returned in January 1966 to find the Adamian mess in my bailiwick. Looking at what had occurred, and feeling that the whole idea of a loyalty oath was wrong (it was later declared unconstitutional by the Oregon State Supreme Court), I sympathized with Adamian. I went to the president, arguing that the dismissal letter should be withdrawn. I insisted that a meeting be scheduled and that I be present. Adamian had become extremely contentious—even using his classes to preach his cause—

but he agreed to meet with Stevenson. In the end, Stevenson said he would revoke his letter of dismissal if Adamian would cease his complaints and outcries to off-campus organizations such as the ACLU and AAUP. Adamian agreed, and the two shook hands. A week later, Adamian violated the agreement by going to the ACLU again. Stevenson reinstated the dismissal, and I could only concur with him. Adamian obtained a position at the University of Nevada, Reno, though he was later fired from that job, too.

The second great event of 1966 had to do with the Mosser Plan. State Representative John Mosser had convinced the 1965 legislature to pass his bill for a Faculty Merit Program. The idea was to reward good undergraduate instruction at the state institutions. Faculty selected for the award would receive $1,000 each. At SOC, eleven such awards were to be given, out of a faculty of 182. Though the selection process was not specified by the legislature, it was clear that the winning faculty should be chosen by the students. Working with the administration, the Faculty Council appointed a committee whose task was to design a student questionnaire. The group worked for almost nine months to produce a questionnaire that would minimize popularity and emphasize educational results. It was administered to students in early 1966, and the results were announced in April. The winners were Julian Battaile (Chemistry), Richard Byrns (English), Claude Curran (Geography), Michael Haynes (Economics), Douglas Legg (History), William Meulemans (Political Science), Clifford Miller (History), Richard Welton (Biology), Arnold Wolfe (Business), Man He You (Economics), and me (Humanities). Not one of these individuals was known as an easy grader. We all insisted on hard work from our students and held high standards. Predictably, the results made a great many hard-working faculty members unhappy, and SOC discontinued the Mosser Plan Awards.

Keith Allison (left) at Mt. Ashland in 1966

That brings us to our third great event of 1966: the Faculty Revolt. Established in 1956 with seven members, the Faculty Council comprised thirteen members by 1965. This body had been growing increasingly unhappy with Stevenson, although he seemed unaware of any problems. Indeed, he again reported to the board, "faculty spirit is good." The central problem had to do with growth. Since arriving, Stevenson had taken command of all aspects of the School's administration. He knew where everyone was, what the problems were, and what to do. That worked well in a small school. He was able to run it out of his vest pocket, so to speak. But SOC had grown substantially larger over the years. Stevenson did not seem to realize that with more than 3,000 students, no single person could run the entire institution. Suddenly, the whole affair exploded on him.

In early April 1966, the entire Faculty Council resigned. The resignation was published in the *Siskiyou*, and all thirteen members of the council signed their names. This was a group of outstanding individuals. Seven of them were department heads. All of them were held in high regard by the faculty, who had elected them in the first place. The resignations came as a great shock to many. The council was forthright in stating the reason for their resignation: They could no longer accept being ignored by the administration, which did not listen to their recommendations and took actions without their knowledge or consent. They felt useless and slighted.

The result was the administration's awakening. They recognized the need for a new faculty constitution, which would provide for an empowered Faculty Senate modeled after the faculty senate at the University of Oregon. The administration presented the new constitution to the faculty in early June 1966. It was approved by the administration and 82 percent of the faculty. The constitution created a Faculty Senate comprising twenty members, fourteen from Southern Oregon College's departments, and six who could be from any department.

In his 1966 year-end report to the board, Stevenson said SOC was still helping the Oregon Shakespeare Festival and Britt Festivals and that it continued to have a need for more buildings, land, and money for instruction, research, and higher salaries. The faculty numbered 182, of which 66 percent were men, 40 percent held doctorates, 19 percent were professors, 15 percent were associate professors, 45 percent were assistant professors, and 21 percent were instructors. The average age was forty-two. The civil service workers now numbered 145. The student-teacher ratio stood at 23:1, and it was time, Stevenson concluded, for the Institution to receive university status.

Swedenburg House

In 1966–67, the new library building opened and the four Green-springs dormitories were completed. Bells rang out across campus, marking the hours, thanks to the donation of a carillon by Ed Rountree, publisher of the *Ashland Daily Tidings*. A degree program in law enforcement (later criminology) was initiated under Eldon Dunn, a retired FBI agent. The departmental title "head" changed to "chairman."

The College acquired the Swedenburg House this academic year. Now called the Plunkett Center, the Swedenburg House had been the residence of Dr. Genevieve Swedenburg, who served as a physician at the College in addition to her private practice. Upon her death, the property came to SOC. Renovated in the 1970s, it currently houses the SOU Foundation and Alumni Office.

Since it no longer served as the library, Central Hall was remodeled the following year. Science Building Two also went into service, greatly expanding the scientific facilities. The director of business affairs became "dean of administration." A Library Science Department was organized, as was a program in nursing. Bachelor's degrees were approved for physics and sociology-anthropology.

It was in 1968–69 that KSOR became the College radio station. Degree programs in economics, political science, and speech (later communication) were first offered. Chairmanships were appointed in the Departments of Economics, Geography, Law Enforcement, Physics, Political Science, Psychology, and Sociology. A master's degree program in outdoor education was established.

James K. Sours

After twenty-three years of service, President Stevenson retired. A faculty search committee worked for more than a year to find Stevenson's successor. They finally selected James K. Sours.

Sours was born in Corydon, Iowa, and he attended the University of Wichita, Kansas, where he earned his BA in 1949. He received a PhD from Harvard University in 1954. Sours was a professor of political science at the University of Wichita before becoming the dean of its College of Arts and Sciences in 1962. From 1965 to 1968, he served as executive vice president of the American College Testing Program in Iowa City. In 1968–69, he was the Fulbright visiting professor of political science at the University of Istanbul, Turkey.

President Sours's first year (1969–70) began with an enrollment of 4,432 students, a faculty of 232 members, a campus of 150 acres, and a library of approximately 160,000 volumes. Clearly, the School had

Elmo Stevenson in the Homecoming Parade, 1968

seen a great deal of growth in all areas during the 1960s. In this last year of the decade, the Sociology Department became the Sociology-Anthropology Department. The Faculty Senate passed a motion to ensure that all future departmental and divisional chairs would be elected by their constituents, rather than appointed by the administration. This was approved by President Sours.

Throughout the 1960s, tuition had been rising, slowly but inexorably. Back in 1959, undergraduate tuition per term was $62 for Oregon residents and $97 for nonresidents. By 1972, tuition stood at $136 for resident undergraduates and $359 for nonresident undergraduates. Because the state legislature had repeatedly reduced funding, Oregon colleges had been forced to increase tuition rates to cover operating costs. Needless to say, no one liked this, least of all the students. Living and book costs were rising as well. Room and board had gone from around $200 per term in 1959–60 to around $400 per term in 1970–71.

BECOMING A UNIVERSITY

THE 1970s

IN 1970–71, A BACCALAUREATE DEGREE in geography was approved, as was an interdisciplinary degree in general studies. The title of the Speech Department was changed to Speech Communication and Theatre Arts. For the first time, the role of Education Department chairman was filled by someone other than the dean of education, who had hitherto served both functions. Perhaps the most far-reaching change occurred in the graduation requirements for the BA and BS degrees. The credits required for a degree were reduced from 192 to 186. General education requirements were reduced to 63 credits, the physical education requirement was eliminated, and the writing requirement was reduced from 9 to 6 credits.

The following year, the Health and Physical Education Division was reorganized, and three departments were created within it:

Professional Preparation, Health Education, and Basic Instruction. Perhaps the most exciting event was the completion of the new student union, which was named Stevenson Union upon the death of Elmo Stevenson in 1973.

Also in 1973, the College began offering a BA in Spanish, the Music Building went into service, and Britt Hall was remodeled, since it no longer served as the student union. The Education-Psychology Building also opened its doors in the 1973–74 academic year. Further, 25 acres were added to the campus, bringing the total acreage to 175.

In 1975, the Law Enforcement Department became the Criminology Department, and a BS in nursing was established. That year, the name of the Institution changed yet again, becoming Southern Oregon State College (SOSC).

The next few years were to be years of great change and upset, especially for the administration. On the academic side, three new degree programs were instituted. In 1976–77, SOSC offered an interdisciplinary master's degree and the first interdisciplinary bachelor's degree program, which combined business and chemistry. SOSC also established a degree program in geology. Additionally, the College radio station, KSOR, went from being a 10-watt station to a 2,000-watt station, enabling it to reach out to the whole Rogue Valley.

On the negative side, there was a serious budget crisis, which called for reductions in excess of $200,000. It was at this point that President Sours declared he would resign his position at the end of 1979. Before leaving, however, he reorganized the entire upper level administration. In response to his wishes, all three academic deans—the dean of faculty, the dean of arts and sciences, and the dean of education—resigned. Some faculty referred to this episode as "the great massacre" of 1977. In their discussions, however, the deans had made it clear to the president that they felt they were serving as deans only upon his sufferance. All of them had tenure as full professors, and their salaries continued. They were treated well, and each was old enough to retire within a few years.

The administration then established a new position, dean of academic affairs, which was filled in January 1978 by Ernest Ettlich. Having earned his BS at Los Angeles State College, Ettlich obtained both an MS and a PhD at the University of Oregon. Ettlich was dean of faculty and vice president at Westmont College before arriving at SOSC in 1978.

President Sours submitted his resignation as of December 31, 1978. A faculty search committee quickly began looking for a new president.

Ernest Ettlich

In the 1977–78 academic year, the College approved a master's degree in business administration. That was an important event, as students in the business programs were beginning to outnumber students in the education programs, and, consequently, the nature of the Institution was changing. SOSC was no longer essentially a normal school, but it was developing all of the attributes of a small university.

Natalie Sicuro

The efforts of the presidential search committee resulted in the appointment of Natalie Sicuro as the new president of Southern Oregon State College. Dr. Sicuro was born in Walden, Ohio. He earned his BS from Kent State University in 1957, an MS from the University of North Carolina in 1958, and a PhD at Kent State in 1964. He served as a teacher and coach in Ohio schools between 1958 and 1962. From 1956 to 1972, he was the as-

KSOR in 1977

sistant dean of the regional Kent State campuses, and in 1972, he became dean of continuing education and associate provost at Kent State. He took office at SOSC on January 1, 1979.

That same year, the SOSC wrestling team won the NAIA National Wrestling Championship under Coach Robert Riehm.

President Sicuro immediately instituted a number of changes at the Institution. He insisted that the College be called "Southern" in its short form, and he quickly changed what were called "Divisions" to "Schools." SOSC now had Schools of Business, Education-Psychology, Health and Physical Education, Humanities, Science-Mathematics, and Social Science.

By the end of the 1970s, enrollment had not changed much; there were 4,443 students in 1979, compared with 4,432 in 1969. Faculty had grown to 247. The library collection had risen to 180,000 volumes. The campus acreage stood at 175. Tuition, however, had more than doubled; it was now $286 per term for residents and $891 per term for nonresidents.

THE 1980s

The 1980s began on an upbeat note. The College was granted a chapter of the national honor society Phi Kappa Phi (PKP). Also, the Theatre Arts Building opened its doors, and a Computer Center was established in the basement of Britt. Computer science was added to the Mathematics Department curriculum. Finally, an Elderhostel Program was organized at the College. Bringing in older and retired people from all over the country, the seniors program quickly became the largest such program in the United States at that time.

The following year, the Center for Continuing Education expanded and was given a home of its own in Siskiyou Hall, as well as a director and a mandate to offer a variety of courses to the entire seven-county region of southern Oregon and northern California. At that same time, studies in speech, journalism, and broadcasting were combined into a Department of Communication.

President Sicuro especially valued athletics. He was quite unhappy with the available spectator facilities on the athletics grounds at Fuller Field. As a result, he decided to build Raider Stadium, which opened in 1983. One of his rewards that year came when SOSC's wrestling team won the School's second NAIA National Championship.

On the academic side, SOSC began offering a BFA in art, plus two new comajors in business-mathematics and business-music. The College set up the School of Fine and Performing Arts, comprising the Art, Music, and Theatre Arts and Dance Departments. Thus, there were now seven schools in the College, each headed by a director.

Perhaps the most important event of the 1983–84 academic year was the development of a BA/BS program in computer science. This was to have vital consequences for the Institution. From then on, computers began springing up all over campus.

In 1984–85, the Computer Science and Mathematics Departments were removed from the School of Science-Mathematics and organized as the School of Computer Information Systems. Nursing was also removed from Science and became a school in its own right. The Institution now had nine schools, not counting graduate programs. At that same time, two new programs were added in the School of Social Science: international studies and women's studies. Sicuro appointed me College historian, thinking it was time to officially record the history of the Institution. Having retired in 1981, I was delighted at the prospect of tackling this long-term project.

The year 1985–86 saw a great many changes. The State Board of Higher Education selected Sicuro for the presidency at Portland State University. Subsequently, Dean Ettlich was appointed interim president of SOSC, and a search committee was formed to find a new president. The Fine and Performing Arts School organized master's degree programs, and the Schneider Museum of Art opened its doors, thanks to a generous gift from Florence and William Schneider.

Joseph Cox

The search for a new president proceeded swiftly, concluding in early 1987 with the appointment of Joseph Cox. Having earned his BA at the University of Maryland in 1959, Cox began teaching history at Towson State University in Maryland in 1964. He received his PhD from the University of Maryland in 1967, becoming a dean at Towson State in 1975. Cox served as acting president at Towson State in 1978–79 and vice president for academic affairs from 1979 to 1981. He was also vice president for academic affairs at Northern Arizona University from 1981 to 1987.

After several years of fierce debate among the faculty, SOSC established a military science program in 1987. The program included a Reserve Officer Training Corps (ROTC) option.

Also in 1987, the College acquired the Mary Phipps Center in Medford, enabling SOSC to offer courses in Medford on a regular basis. It was at this time that the College provided land for a new National Guard Armory and the National Fish and Wildlife Forensics Laboratory in Ashland.

An MBA degree in business administration was approved in 1987–88.

MTV VJ Julie Brown visits campus in 1987

The following year saw the start of the Rogue Valley Television Station (RVTV), a cable access TV station organized by the College in cooperation with the city of Ashland and the Ashland Community Hospital.

In 1989, Ernest Ettlich resigned as dean of academic affairs, fulfilling his long-time dream of teaching full time in the Communication Department. The administration appointed Stephen Reno dean of academic affairs in his stead.

The decade closed with an enrollment of 4,470 students, a faculty of 283, and a library collection of about 250,000 volumes. The campus acreage remained stable at 175 acres. Tuition continued to increase, standing at $532 per term for residents and $1,349 for nonresidents.

THE 1990s

With the arrival of the 1990s, there was a strong feeling on campus that SOSC needed reorganization. The administration and the Faculty Senate agreed to employ three consultants to examine SOSC and make recommendations for the Institution's organization. In August 1990, the consultants arrived. They were James Bemis, who had served as executive director of the Commission on Colleges of the Northwest Association of Schools and Colleges for twenty-five years; Edward Kormondy, chancellor of the University of Hawaii; and me (I had spent eight years as a member of the Commission on Colleges, visiting and evaluating more than fifty institutions.). We analyzed the operations of the College, concluding that nine schools were far too many for an institution of this size. The School of Nursing was soon to be transferred from SOSC's governance. We recommended that the remaining eight schools be reduced to four, although there was some thought that two would be even better. Over the next several years, our basic recommendation was accepted and implemented.

In 1990–91, the College began three new BA/BS degree programs in fine and performing arts, health and physical education, and computer science and mathematics. There were also two new MA/MS degree programs in environmental education and mathematical and computer sciences. McNeal Hall received an addition, as did Stevenson Union, which now housed the College Bookstore. On the lower campus, the College developed Old Mill Village, a student family housing complex. With 130 apartment units, the complex occupies seven acres.

The following year, the Computer Services Building opened. The College radio station, KSOR, became Jefferson Public Radio (JPR). SOSC's nine schools were reduced to five. The School of Sciences absorbed Computer Science and Mathematics, while Humanities and Fine and Performing Arts joined the School of Arts and Letters. Nursing and Health temporarily added Health and Physical Education, and Education and Psychology became part of the School of Social Science. At the same time, the directors of the schools were renamed deans.

In 1992–93, the nursing program shifted to Oregon Health Sciences University (OHSU) and became its School of Nursing at Southern Oregon State College. Health and Physical Education moved to the School of Social Science and Education, further reducing SOSC's schools to four. Also in 1993, the College inaugurated Southern Oregon Learning in Retirement (SOLIR), a program for local senior citizens that quickly became popular. SOSC also appointed a special consultant for affirmative action to the general administration. This position had been filled during the 1980s, was omitted for three years at the beginning of the 1990s, and was later dropped in 1998.

The year 1993 was the last time the College published its annual yearbook, the *Raider*. The yearbook had been losing money, and the student body lacked the interest to keep it going.

The 1993–94 academic year was eventful. When the position of chancellor of the Oregon State System of Higher Education fell vacant, the state board appointed SOSC President Joseph Cox to the position on an interim basis. At the same time, the board appointed Stephen Reno (then provost and dean of faculty) interim president of SOSC. The new associate provost, Sara Hopkins-Powell, filled the provost position. There were now four schools, and an associate dean for education was appointed in the School of Social Science and Education. The administration then hired a new special assistant to the president, who would also serve as the affirmative action coordinator.

In 1994, SOSC's wrestling team won its third NAIA National Wrestling Championship. This was also the year when the Pacific Northwest Museum of Natural History opened its doors on the lower campus, realizing the long-time dream of Emeritus Biology Professor Ronald Lamb. Unfortunately, funding problems developed after a few years of operation, and the museum had to close its doors in 1997.

Stephen J. Reno

Both Joseph Cox's position as chancellor and Stephen Reno's position as president became permanent in 1995. Consequently, Sara Hopkins-Powell was appointed provost and dean of faculty, and Charles Lane became the associate provost. Now called the ACCESS Center, the Student Services Center opened in Stevenson Union. The Physical Plant offices moved to new quarters on the lower campus; their old facility was remodeled and turned into a sculpture studio for the Art Department.

Sara Hopkins-Powell

The next great event for the Institution occurred on April 1, 1997, when Governor John Kitzhaber signed the bill transforming Southern Oregon State College into Southern Oregon University. At long last, what had been true of the Institution for many years received official recognition. The following year, SOU updated its athletic logo for the Raiders, introducing the red-tailed hawk.

The SOU Foundation conducted a fundraising program for the Center for the Visual Arts (CVA), bringing in $11.6 million, which included a matching grant of $5.6 million from the legislature. Following this successful fundraising effort, SOU began construction of the CVA in front of the Schneider Museum.

Center for the Visual Arts

In July 2000, President Reno resigned, accepting an appointment as chancellor of New Hampshire's institutions of higher education. On the recommendation of Chancellor Cox, the State Board of Higher Education appointed Sara Hopkins-Powell interim president of SOU. Hopkins-Powell received a BS degree from Ohio State, as well as MPH and PhD degrees from the University of California, Berkeley. Having arrived at SOSC in 1993 as the associate provost, Hopkins-Powell had become provost when Reno assumed the presidency.

On the advice of the Faculty Senate, Hopkins-Powell appointed Neil Kunze interim provost during her presidency. Kunze had been the interim dean of arts and letters, a position that would be permanently filled by Edwin Battistella, who arrived in summer 2000.

In spring 2000, a search committee was appointed to find a new president. The committee was headed by Bill Williams, chief executive officer of the Bear Creek Corporation and a leading member of the State Board of Higher Education.

Center for the Visual Arts grand opening celebration in October 2000

Later that summer, Jon Mitchell, former president of the Asante Health System, was named vice president for university relations and executive director of the Southern Oregon University Foundation.

In October 1999, the Center for the Visual Arts was dedicated in an impressive grand opening ceremony, bringing Reno back to campus for the occasion. Some parts of the center were still under construction, but the Marion Ady Building was complete. Marion Ady had been a beloved professor of art in the early days of the Institution. One of the original faculty members in 1926, Ady was the first chair of the Art Department, which she had in effect founded. The sculpture studio, formerly called Art East, was re-christened the DeBoer Sculpture Building in honor of Walter DeBoer, an early supporter.

THE
TWENTY-FIRST CENTURY

On March 2, 2001, the Oregon State Board of Higher Education appointed Elisabeth Zinser, chancellor of the University of Kentucky, Lexington, president of Southern Oregon University.

One day later, the SOU wrestling team won its fourth NAIA National Wrestling Championship in St. Charles, Missouri, under the guidance of Coach Michael Ritchey. Jeremy Wynia and John Sills became individual title holders, and ten members of the team were awarded All-American honors.

Elisabeth Zinser

President Zinser took office in August. Zinser received a BS from Stanford University in 1964; MS degrees from the University of California, San Francisco, in 1966 and MIT in 1982; and a PhD from the University of California, Berkeley, in 1972. She was a professor and dean of the College of Nursing at the University of North Dakota from 1977 to 1983 before becoming vice chancellor for academic affairs at the University of North Carolina in 1983. Zinser was elected president of Gallaudet University by its board in 1989. Gallaudet is a famous institution for the deaf, and the students insisted that their president also be a deaf person. Out of respect for the students' wishes, Zinser resigned from office. She then accepted the presidency at the University of Idaho, serving from 1989 to 1995. In 1995, she became chancellor of the University of Kentucky, Lexington. Zinser is Southern Oregon University's tenth president.

THE INSTITUTION IN 1926 AND 2001

1926

SOUTHERN OREGON STATE NORMAL SCHOOL

Enrollment 273

Faculty 11

Library .... 3,500 volumes

Programs .... Two-year elementary program

Campus .... 18 acres

Academic Buildings 1

Residence Halls 0

2001

SOUTHERN OREGON UNIVERSITY

Enrollment 5,772

Faculty 283

Library .... More than 300,000 volumes

Programs .... Thirty-five baccalaureate programs and twelve graduate programs

Campus .... 175 acres

Academic Buildings 13

Residence Halls 14

CODA

FUN AND GAMES
AT THE OLD COLLEGE

DURING THE 1950S AND 1960S, much of the good feeling on campus grew out of the general faculty lounge, where professors could take a break and have coffee with colleagues. The lounge was located on the first floor on the west side of Britt Hall. There, humanities faculty could mingle with science, social science, and education faculty, as well as administrators. It was healthy for faculty to meet socially across departmental lines. The faculty enjoyed this so much that they were willing to raise funds to support the faculty lounge by producing an annual Faculty Follies show in the early 1950s, attracting students and townspeople alike.

One of the campus leaders during this time was Arthur Samuel Taylor, chairman of the Social Science Division. Much loved on campus, he was named "Man of the Year" and "Mr. Southern Oregon College" just before his death in 1963. In 1969, the Social Science building was named Taylor Hall is his honor.

Taylor had a keen sense of humor. For example, when school began each fall, the president would hold a faculty meeting prior to the start of classes. At that meeting, the president customarily asked each faculty member for a report on what they had done during the past summer. Faculty members doggedly rose and told of the trips they had taken. This one had gone to Boston, another to New York, one went to Paris, another to London, and so on until it was Arthur Taylor's turn. He rose and described, in excruciating detail, his trip to Talent. We were rolling in the aisles doubled over with laughter before he was through.

Perhaps Taylor's most memorable creation was a faculty men's group, which he named the Birdwatcher Society. This group began meeting in 1950 and lasted until Taylor's death. The men met for lunch every Wednesday at noon in the Susanne Homes Hall cafeteria. It had nothing whatever to do with ornithology. The "bird" we were watching was our president, Elmo Stevenson. All who came to the lunch contributed a dime to a kitty, and the man who drew the highest card from a deck of pornographic playing cards (contributed by a member who shall remain nameless here) won the kitty. Some of the members were also given fanciful titles. For instance, the office of Ultimate Oblivion went to the person who had entered a doctoral program but was furthest from achieving it. It was all great, innocent fun.

Arthur Samuel Taylor

An amusing sidenote to all of this occurred in 1955. That year, I was appointed a Ford Foundation Scholar at Harvard University. I also had a nephew who was a printer. While in Boston, I had a series of letterheads printed for the various universities I was planning to visit on my way home from Harvard (e.g., University of Virginia, Duke University, Tulane University). The Harvard letterhead was typical. It read, "The Birdwatcher Society of Harvard University." At Harvard, I had a small office near where the famous American historian Oscar Handlin worked. Arthur Taylor taught American history at SOSC—so I sent him a letter on the Birdwatcher letterhead, saying how pleased Harvard was to follow his lead in setting up such a society, signed by Oscar Handlin! Shortly after, Dr. Handlin paid me a visit, asking if I was from Southern Oregon, and who the hell was Dr. Taylor. I explained what I was doing, and he laughed and left. I repeated this performance on the

Marion Ady

long trip back to Ashland, with letterheads from all of the universities. When I reached Ashland, Taylor was beside himself with joy over the great spread of the Birdwatchers, and then I had to confess to what I had done. What a blow.

Not to be outdone, the faculty women—regarding the Birdwatchers as a sexist group—formed an organization of their own. In 1957, they came together to form the United Foundation Trust (UFT), or Uftuddies. It wasn't long, however, before they became known as The Order of the Purple Girdle. They had regular dinner meetings in member's homes, and the meetings were conducted by the "Main Stay," later called the President in Perpetuity. That was Marion Ady. (The UFT seems to have ended with Ady's retirement in 1964.) Whenever a member achieved a doctorate, there was a girdling ceremony for her. The members were all given titles: the first vice president was the Zipper-Upper, the secretary was the Eye, and the treasurer was the Hook. All of the members were second vice presidents, and each had a name, such as Hinder Binder, Cumber Bun, Wasp Waist, Kitten Hips, and Maiden Form. The meetings were based on invented nonsense, and discussing school business was frowned on. They displayed a great deal of humor and had a lot of fun. All in all, it must be said, they were considerably funnier and more artistic than the men.

NOTES ON WOMEN AT SOUTHERN OREGON

WHEN THE THIRD INCARNATION of the College began in 1926, it was a two-year institution for the preparation of elementary school teachers. That year, females comprised more than 76 percent of the faculty, 88 percent of the student body, and 91 percent of the graduates (obviously, many had prior academic preparation).

Henrietta Hall

Given these overwhelming percentages, it is both fascinating and baffling to note that the elected president and vice president of the student body were men. The presidents of the senior and junior classes were men. Even the editor and business manager of the *Siskiyou* were men.

Although a woman (Helen Lyons) became student body president briefly in 1928—she was vice president and stepped up when the male president resigned—the first elected female student body president, Henrietta Hall, did not take office until 1943. That, of course, was during World War II, and the College's enrollment was down to fifty-nine students. Of these, nine were men, and many were townspeople who enrolled in the odd course just to help keep the College's numbers up.

Although only thirty-one men enrolled in 1926, the School formed a men's varsity basketball team. There was a women's chorus, but the men's chorus disbanded after a few months. There was a men's debate team; a women's team was proposed, but it never got off the ground.

As mentioned earlier, there was a riding club comprising thirty-two women and a coed rifle club (eighteen men and seventy-five women). The women of those days could ride and shoot! A women's hiking club was organized the following year, and the Institution agreed to grant the athletic award of college letters to qualified women. The requirements were rigorous: Women had to hike more than 120 miles in the season. This included several stipulated difficult climbs, as well as at least three overnight treks. By the end of 1928, twenty-seven women had received letters. This continued into the 1930s.

Another mark of honor for women was the 1932 purchase (with assistance of a Carnegie Foundation grant) of the memorial plaque, "Pioneer Woman," which was hung in the entrance to the College (now Churchill Hall). The plaque is currently on display in the University Library.

As soon as the 1926 term began, it became clear there was a desperate need for a woman's dormitory. Recommended by all, a bill calling for a women's dormitory was passed by the legislature. The governor, however, vetoed it on the grounds that there was no money appropriated. A gymnasium was built in 1936 with federal funds, but the women's dorm did not become a reality until 1947. The hall is named for Susanne Homes, an 1896 graduate of the old normal school (the second incarnation: Southern Oregon State Normal School, 1895–1909). Homes became the Jackson County superintendent of schools.

The percentage of enrolled women declined regularly until it hit a low of 31 percent in 1946, probably caused by the wave of men returning from military service who rushed to take advantage of the GI Bill. Not until the 1990s did women students become a majority again (in 1990 at 54.7 percent).

Women faculty percentages declined even more precipitously, dropping to 19.3 percent in 1976, then beginning a slow climb upward. With the arrival of President Cox in 1987, women faculty increased by a healthy 8 percent, and by 1991, the overall percentage of women faculty had reached almost 35 percent. The University still had a ways to go, but improvement has been marked in recent years. In 2001, the faculty percentage for women reached 41 percent.

By 1981, women were regularly elected to high office and appointed to leading positions, such as editor of the *Siskiyou*.

Below are the names and years of service of some of the female student body presidents:

Monica Cozza, 1988

Ann Meredith, 1989

Farah Jackson, 1990

Amanda Smith, 1992

Sophia McDonald, 1998

Betsy Fox, 1999

Tamara Henderson, 2001

Leanne Armstrong, Dianne Gotman, Rae Lester, and Tammy Lindsley were the last editors of the College yearbooks from 1989 until publication ceased in 1993.

Siskiyou editors-in-chief from 1990 to 2002 included Lea Connor, Larissa Holloway, LaVerne Walentine, Tiffany Coleman, Jessica Smith, Jill McDaniel, Sara Murphy, Joanne Collins, and Jennifer Squires.

Beverly Bennett

Robert Bennett

Vaughn Bornet

Angus Bowmer

Harold Cloer

Joseph Cox

Rosemary Dunn
Dalton

Betty Lou Dunlop

Ronald Kramer

Arthur Kreisman

Ronald Lamb

Donald Laws

Roy McNeal

Loren Messenger

Alexander Petersen

Dean Phelps

Gary Prickett

Margaret Skerry

Elmo Stevenson

Marshall Woodell

COMMUNITY CONTRIBUTIONS

MANY MEMBERS of the academic community have made important contributions far beyond their institutional service, and they are well worth remembering. This will inevitably be an incomplete list, and I apologize to those who have been accidentally omitted.

Les AuCoin, Visiting Professor of Political Science. Served in the Oregon House of Representatives, 1971–74. Elected to the U.S. Congress in 1976 and served with distinction until 1992.

Beverly Bennett, Professor of Physical Education. Helped start the Jackson County Special Olympics program in the 1950s.

Robert Bennett, Dean of Men. Served on the Ashland Parks and Recreation Commission, 1968–78 and 1995–99.

Beth Bornet. Served on the Ashland Community Hospital Foundation Board in the 1980s.

Vaughn Bornet, Professor of Social Science. Served on the U.S. Civil Rights Commission for Oregon in 1985.

Photographs unavailable for Les AuCoin, Beth Bornet, Evelyn Kreisman,
Leonard Levy, John Trudeau, and Robert Winthrop

Angus Bowmer, Professor of Drama. Founded the Oregon Shakespeare Festival in the 1930s. Produced outdoor plays beginning in 1935, gradually developing an Elizabethan theater that achieved national recognition. For details of his story, see Bowmer's autobiography, *As I Remember, Adam,* published by the Oregon Shakespearean Festival Association in 1975.

Harold Cloer, Professor of Psychology. Received the prestigious Ragland Memorial Community Service Award in 2001 from the Ashland City Council. The award was in recognition for his forty years of volunteer work for various organizations and city projects.

Joseph Cox, President of SOSC. Appointed chancellor of the Oregon State System of Higher Education in 1994.

Rosemary Dunn Dalton, SOSC graduate student. A key figure in assisting abused women. Helped found the Dunn House, 1977–81.

Betty Lou Dunlop, Professor of Education. Served on the Ashland School Board, 1982–84.

Ronald Kramer, Executive Director of Jefferson Public Radio. Took over radio station KSOR in 1974, greatly increasing its power and reach in 1976. Transformed KSOR into Jefferson Public Radio (JPR) in 1991.

Arthur Kreisman, Professor of Humanities. Served on the Ashland City Council, 1950–54. Commander of the Ashland Post of the American Legion and founder of the Rogue Valley Unitarian Universalist Fellowship. Named editor of *The Oregon Centennial Anthology* on the occasion of Oregon's hundredth anniversary in 1959. Also a founder and the first chairman of the Ashland Community Hospital Board, 1960–62.

Evelyn Kreisman. First president of the combined Ashland Parent-Teachers Associations and the first chairperson of the Ashland Community Hospital Foundation in 1977.

Ronald Lamb, Professor of Biology. Founded the ill-fated Pacific Northwest Museum of Natural History in 1993.

Donald Laws, Professor of Political Science. Served on the Ashland City Council continuously from 1975 to 2000.

Leonard Levy, Adjunct Professor of History and Political Science, Distinguished Scholar in Residence. Winner of the 1969 Pulitzer Prize in History for his book, *Origins of the Fifth Amendment.* Nationally known author, editor, and contributor to scholarly endeavors.

Roy McNeal, Professor of Geography. Grandmaster of the Oregon Masons, 1954–55.

Loren Messenger, Professor of Psychology. A naval officer who had to leave the faculty when the U.S. entered World War II. His last naval assignment was as commandant of Kingsley Field in Klamath Falls.

Alexander Petersen, Professor of Physical Education. One of the founders of the Rogue Valley Swim and Tennis Club in 1959.

Dean Phelps, Professor of Geography. Served on the Ashland City Council, 1977–80.

Gary Prickett, Professor of Business and Dean of Development. Served as mayor of Ashland, 1975–80.

Margaret Skerry (Maggie Bolton), Director of Dormitories. Served on the Ashland Community Hospital Board of Directors in the late 1970s and early 1980s.

Elmo Stevenson, President of SOC. In 1968, he became director of the Rogue Valley Manor, which he had helped found ten years earlier.

John Trudeau, Assistant Professor of Music. Visiting SOC for the summer sessions from 1963 to 1968, Trudeau founded Britt Festivals. He was greatly aided in that endeavor by Herbert Cecil, head of the SOC Department of Music.

Robert Winthrop, Adjunct Professor of Anthropology. Served on the Ashland City Council, 1989–95.

Marshall Woodell, Professor of Political Science and Graduate Dean. Served on the Ashland City Council, 1940–41, and the Ashland School Board, 1950–53.

Robert Casebeer   *James Dawson*   *Betty Haugen*   *Irene Hollenbeck*

Ronald Lamb   *Leon Mulling*   *Lloyd Pennington*   *Robert Riehm*

OUTSTANDING FACULTY
CONTRIBUTIONS

OVER THE YEARS, faculty members have made a great variety of significant contributions to the Institution and the community. Below are a few whose work deserves special mention.

Robert Casebeer, Associate Professor of English. Served from 1964 to 1993. In 1965, Casebeer conceived the idea of assisting the development of gifted students in the region, and he submitted a proposal to the government that was funded under the National Education Act. Called Project Prometheus, it provided full-fee scholarships to 200 students from forty-eight high schools in the seven southern Oregon counties. There were twenty faculty involved, as well as outstanding national lecturers. They engaged in six-week programs during the summers of 1966, 1967, and 1968. Casebeer directed the highly successful project.

James Dawson, Professor of Biology. Came to the College in 1956 and died while still in service in 1965. A dynamic and much-loved instructor, he was greatly concerned about students with disabilities, especially those who were blind. He developed special teaching aids to help blind students learn biology.

Betty Haugen, Professor of Nursing. Served from 1967 to 1985. Almost single-handedly created the Nursing Department at the College. In 1967, she first set up an associate degree program that produced registered nurses. She then added courses and faculty to build the program to baccalaureate-degree status by 1975.

Irene Hollenbeck, Professor of Science and Education. Served from 1954 to 1972. Included in *Who's Who in American Education,* Hollenbeck was active in her profession. In 1958, she was elected president of the National Association of Biology Teachers. She served as director of a National Science Foundation Institute held at Southern Oregon College in 1961 to improve the teaching of general science at the junior-high–school level. Students attended from twenty-one states and one foreign country. Her impact on the teaching of science was such that after her retirement in 1972, the Forest Service in the Rogue River National Forest set up the Hollenbeck Environmental Study Area.

Ronald Lamb, Professor of Biology. Served from 1964 to 1989. In 1983, he developed a master's degree program in outdoor education, which became the environmental education program in 1990. That same year, he began work on the Pacific Northwest Museum of Natural History, which was built on Walker Avenue and East Main Street. It operated for several years before closing in 1997 due to financial problems.

Leon Mulling, Professor of Speech-Communication. Served from 1946 to 1979. Developed a speech clinic for youth. Contributed significantly to the creation of the Center for the Visual Arts. He also gave generously for student scholarships over the years.

Lloyd Pennington, Professor of Chemistry. Served from 1946 to 1979. Was responsible for creating the Chemistry Department under difficult conditions. He developed the first chemistry laboratory, located in the basement of the old gymnasium (before it was rebuilt as Britt Hall). In 1955, he obtained the first grant for science research at the College.

Robert Riehm, Associate Professor of Health Education. Served from 1969 to 1995. An outstanding wrestling coach, Riehm led his teams to national championships in 1979, 1983, and 1994—a truly enviable record.

ABOUT THE AUTHOR

Arthur Kreisman, University Historian and Professor Emeritus

Hired by SOCE President Elmo Stevenson in 1946

During his fifty-six–year career at the Institution, Arthur Kreisman has served as professor of both English and German, director of general studies, dean of humanities, dean of arts and sciences, director of curricular affairs, and University historian.

In the community, Kreisman has served as the first chairman of the board for Ashland Community Hospital, founded the local Unitarian Fellowship, sat on the city council (1950–54), and spearheaded numerous educational programs.

His column, "Remembering," appears in Southern Oregon University's alumni magazine, the *Southern Oregonian*.